Why I'm Against

It All

RANTS & REFLECTIONS

Why I'm Against It All

It All

Rants & Reflections

Ken Wright

Raven's Eye Press

Raven's Eye Press, Inc.
P.O. Box 4351
Durango, CO 81302-4544

Essays in this book have previously appeared in the following places: *Canoe & Kayak, Colorado Central, Inside/Outside Southwest, Mountainfreak, Rocky Mountain News, San Juan Almanac, Telluride Magazine,* and "Writers on the Range" (a syndicated column from *High Country News*).

Wright, Ken
    Why I'm against it all: rants and reflections/Ken Wright
    p. cm.
1. Nature Writing 2. Environment
3. American Southwest
I.Title

Library of Congress Control Number:2003 091332 ©2003
ISBN 0-9700044-2-7 (pbk.:alk. Paper)

Cover design by Todd Thompson
Book Design by Todd Thompson and Raven's Eye Press, Inc.
Cover Photo: Paul Pennington
Author Photo: Sarah Wright

Printed in the United States of America
1 3 5 7 9 10 8 6 4 2

To order this book or to correspond with the author, contact:
RAVEN'S EYE PRESS, INC. PO BOX 4351 DURANGO CO 81302
Individual copies $14.95 plus shipping. Raven's Eye Press books are available at quantity discount. Visit our website at www.ravenseyepress.com

To Sarah,
who has lived through it all,
embraced most of it,
and put up with
the rest.

Content

Why I'm Against It All

Wild People, Unite!

Just say no, No, NO!

The Monkey Wrench Dad

Acknowledgements

The essays collected in this book were written over a period of years, for a number of publications, inspired by a wide variety of occasions, occurrences, opportunities, moods, outrages, musings, offerings, and incidents. They have been modified somewhat to fit and flow together and to articulate some sort of point of view.

You don't have to agree with everything written in here, and no one in their right mind would expect anyone to do everything suggested or implied — these are just my own ravings. So do and think what you think best. As long as you act on whatever it is you yourself believe. Because that's what it's all about, *compañeros*.

I would like to thank the following people for their support, inspiration, conversation, mixology, and/or general spiritual guidance: Sarah, of course, Janet and Matt Kenna, Leigh and Steve Meigs, Scott and Ayla Moore, Todd Thompson, Nancy Jacques, Phil Lauro, Corri Vigil, Mark Seis, David Feela, Pete Prendergast, Kate Niles, Orion the Hunter, and all the river rats and town dogs too numerous to name. And to the kids: Tig, Abi, Ben, Jackson, Maddie, Jack, and, especially, Webb and Anna. Also, thanks to Gregory Moore for the poem "Aftermath" in the essay "Seeing the light after the fire," and to Paul Pennington for the cover photograph.

You all rock.

Why I'm Against It All

Civilization be dinged! —
It is the mountains and the desert for me.

— Ambrose Bierce

Why I'm against it all

For two years I wrote an environmental column for a small western-Colorado newspaper. It wasn't hard work, really. I just rambled on for 600 words each week about the rugged landscape around us and then offered some helpful observations and suggestions: that housing developments really aren't good elk habitat, that the local ski area is big enough already, that the U.S. Forest Service shouldn't execute one of the area's last old-growth Ponderosa stands, that the Bureau of Reclamation shouldn't insert yet another concrete suppository in yet another nearby river, and so on.

Believe it or not, some of those columns drew complaints.

Most of the complaints began with the same general introduction: "Hey you (insert your favorite noun here), you weren't born here, were you?" I appreciated the time folks took to offer me feedback in those notes (sometimes with painstakingly cut-out and taped-on letters) and phone calls (often after midnight, when the rates are low). It also connected me to the many other vocal "newcomers" who have migrated to the West and dared to point out the waste, stupidity, and greed dismantling this fantastic place.

Still, I'm not afraid to admit I wasn't born a Westerner. And I am not afraid to admit — as even many "environmentalists" are for fear of weakening their credibility — that I am against most of the changes happening here: bigger airports, new roads, the widening and straightening and grading of old roads, Wal-Marts, K-marts, mini malls, corporate resorts, ski-area expansions, water developments, golf courses, casinos, marinas, campgrounds, trail-head parking, brochures, maps, promotional websites, and about anything any chamber of commerce anywhere ever does. And so on. Propose it and I oppose it.

I say, stop it all. Keep the roads a mess, the infrastructure archaic, the water scarce and the transportation hell. Don't let the profiteers gouge out the amenities and infrastructure luring the urban refugees now ravaging the West, and they won't come. With every incremental "improvement" in the West, there are a dozen people for whom that improvement makes it just easy enough to live here. And once they get settled, they know it would be perfect if their new town only had a (you name it). And that new improvement just makes it comfortable enough for the next dozen, who just wish their new town (you name it again).

I'm not saying we should shut the door — I moved here, after all. I just say, anyone can live here if they want, as long as they're willing to do it on this place's terms. If folks don't want to give up nice roads, easy access to air transport, bluegrass lawns, tee-times, specialty coffee shops, shopping malls and on-ramps to the information superhighway, then there's most of the rest of the country already paved over, roaded through, and wired-up for them.

I know. I used to live there.

Like many native Westerners, there's a class of us newcomers who love small working towns and wild and undeveloped country. Call us rural refugees. We're from different states, but we're from the same state of mind. We worship the precious backcountry and close-knit communities that still survive in the West, and we settled here willing to sacrifice urban conveniences, high-tech luxuries, and fat paychecks to have those things. We would've been happy to stay wherever we're from, but we saw our native rural towns and landscapes crushed by the glassy-eyed cult of economics that chants "growth is good" and whose vision extends only to the end of the next fiscal year.

And so I say to the long-time lovers of the West who resent *all* newcomers, if you listen to us new lovers of the West we can offer valuable, hard-earned lessons that you'll never hear from a politician, real-estate developer, chain-store corporation or mega-resort. We learned the hard way that you can't have it both ways. We know the planning, studying, sloganeering ("Smart Growth" is Colorado's favorite platitude), mitigation and fire-and-brimstone sermons about the free-market and private property only soothe your conscience and cut loose the profiteers; they do nothing to stop the strip mining of culture and countryside that is the inevitable cost of growth.

That's why we loud-mouth newcomers can't keep quiet when we hear again the familiar optimistic and hypnotic hymns: Growth is good ... We can control growth ... We'll all get rich ... Just a little more improvement ... There's another valley over the ridge, and another river over the hill.

And that is why I'm against it all.

The mountain difference

*A*nother late October afternoon. Today, in spite of the fall warmth, I can look from my front yard and see snow in the Colorado high country, a lacy white shawl over the muscular fall-brown shoulders of the Sierra La Plata. Just the sight of those snowy peaks, even from this warm valley, shoots me a jolt of adrenaline. The hair on my skin rises in a mammalian Pavlovian response, my body suddenly grows restless, instinctively pumping itself up in anticipation of taking on the challenge of the mountains in winter.

I am not alone in this reaction.

Several years ago I was in Innsbruck, in the Austrian Alps. A friend and I had just arrived on an overnight train on which we had spent a long night sleeping on a dirty floor, and I was now tired and grouchy and wanting a place to lounge for a few days. We were picked up at the train station by an older woman who ran a bed and breakfast in the foothills above the city.

As we whipped up the switchbacks out of town, she was not very friendly. That universal sick-of-tourists syndrome, y'know.

"Where you from?" she finally managed to mumble in her heavy Germanic accent.

"The U.S.," I answered. "Colorado."

She glanced at me. Then she smiled at us.

"Mountain people," she said. "We are different."

She catered to us like kin for three days.

Mountain people. We are different. Mountain people perceive and process the world through some older, deeper genetic software because life in the mountains, especially once winter has imposed itself like some kind of climatic martial law, demands a more poised, present, patient, persistent, and prepared attitude just to function. It's not just cold; it's fucking cold. I hitchhiked one morning out of a little town at 9,000 feet at 57 degrees below zero. Not wind chill temperature — there was no wind. There seemed to be no movement at all. Even the wood smoke snaking out of the many cabins and doublewides seemed frozen, immobilized, like absolute zero. As I stood there waiting in the crystalline morning — hoping I wouldn't have to wait too long — snow fell from my breath.

And then there's the real snow. My first winter in Colorado, there was a span in November and December when it snowed non-stop for 28 consecutive days. Years later, I was driving a bus for a ski area, and in an April snowstorm the company snowplow finally surrendered to the heavy and deep over-night accumulation. All but one of 15 got stuck in the parking lot and couldn't get on the road to pick up the gazillion rabid skiers panting to inhale the powder day. That one bus was mine; I quit after my shift.

I still have to drive, though, and when I'm driving over remote mountain passes in the winter I keep in my car a sleeping bag, tire chains, a tow chain, jumper cables, fire-making gear, a shovel, some sand, some food and water. And skiing into the backcountry ... let's say I'm always equipped to at least have a chance at surviving the night. You can't screw around in a land where the day could bury you and the night could kill you.

But mountain people, we are different: the challenges, those risks, and that unforgivingness that must be endured even doing daily chores are what we love. These days, the mountains in winter are the closest we get anymore to a dangerous day-to-day world, like the one humans evolved in. Winter up high is still wild — unharnessed, unpredictable, self-willing, and strong enough to set the rules and punish you if you lose respect. And you can't even hide inside: In Silverton, Colorado, in 1993, snarling blizzards clawed at the upper Animas Valley for two weeks, and even after they retreated, avalanches isolated the town for several more days. Bread and milk had to be flown in by helicopters — when they could — for more than a week.

But as the mountains assert themselves, so do mountain people. The people I know who were in Silverton then say those were a couple of the sweetest weeks in their lives.

In the brief mountain summer, there comes a quick blossoming and softening of the high country. The craggy peaks turn green and wild-flower speckled, the valleys are verdant and threaded with trout-filled creeks, and the relative gentleness of the weather brings out mountain admirers by the millions. But mountain people know the cut is coming: when winter returns home, the mountains again show their true charac-ter. And people theirs — most choose, wisely and with no shame, to leave, to wait for the return of timid and brief summer. The alpine winter is just too dangerous and difficult to endure; it's just too much work and risk for too little reward for most people.

It's a law of human nature: When someplace is difficult to get to and hard to live in, a large segment of the population is filtered out.

For those willing to settle here, then, winter in the mountains shapes their character and forges their culture. An extended tribe arises, its many small bands spread throughout remote mountain towns. Tribes and bands? Why shouldn't this culture be closer to a tribal culture? Built around isolation, challenge, beauty, physical demands, self-reliance, and mutual-aid, mountain-town culture is cut from an environment more akin to what our hunting-and-gathering tribal ancestors experienced. And because of this, mountain people are bound together by having chosen the same demanding lifestyle for the same aesthetic reasons — trading ease, convenience, security, and the economic rewards of the modern world for an older definition of quality of life.

If the history of our dominant modern culture has shown one thing, though, it is that the civilized world is inevitably lethal to tribal cultures everywhere. Mountain town culture in the American West is no exception. Each place writes its own story, but the pattern as it has emerged in the late 20th century is standard: the neo-*conquistadors* in the real-estate offices, travel councils, and chambers of commerce strive to "improve" mountain towns (always for the residents' own good, of course, whether they want to be improved or not) by converting the natives to the "true religion" of economic growth. So here's how a mountain town is killed: The town gets wired to the Great Economy by good roads, tunnels, airports, communications systems, urban amenities, comfortable accommodations, chain stores, and development of some marketable industrial recreation, thereby earning the status of "resort." Then, by sheer economic momentum, the town's population changes. Why? Because that is the definition of a resort: a place offering a lifestyle with enough modern comforts so you can have the style without the demands of the life once required to live there.

If you can afford it, that is.

And those old mountain people? Well, money-making skill was never a priority, or even a necessity, in the mountain-town tribe. In fact, that was the point of the mountain-town culture: to be able get off the great economic Stair Master so you can walk through a deeper, older, more real world out there, still found in the mountains. There's not much money to be made in doing that.

So this is the sad tale unfolding (again) all over the West: habitat for mountain people is endangered as wild mountain towns are domesticated into tourist-farming resorts. It's another rule of human nature: the strip mining of culture is an inevitable cost of the economic benefits of growth.

But here's where the story gets creepy — or encouraging, depending upon your persuasion in these matters: in mountain towns, regardless of how much of a freak show they get turned into (pick your favorite prostituted village: Telluride, Aspen, Breckenridge, Crested Butte, even Vail, although that place is now nearly too sterile to support life as we know it), the mountain-people tribe persists. The town may have been engineered into a fully-fabricated franchised modernized sanitized neutered image-polished jet-serviced on-line interstate-accessible and expensive million-bed year-round destination mega-resort, yet ... yet the mountain people endure like weeds. The most tenacious specimens cling to any crevice in the theme-park pavement available, congregating around a barroom, a sport, an alternative magazine, a small business, or even a river or wilderness area, and forming new communities on some economic reservation somewhere — in a trailer-park hovel or tipi-and-refurbished-school-bus squatters' camp or in the next little mountain town in the next valley over.

You won't see the real mountain people in the chamber of commerce's latest brochure, but they're there, if you care to look. As long as the harshness of the mountains resists complete metroplexing — the goal of today's cult of global economics — then mountain people will endure. As human-ecologist Paul Shepard says, "In defiance of mass culture, tribalism constantly resurfaces."

It's in the genes.

Just look around.

Look for someone standing in his yard and looking up, breathing a little heavily and involuntarily flexing his muscles as he stares out at the season's first high-country snowfall.

Mountain people. We are different.

Going native

"We are Indian. Only part Indian, but it makes a difference."

My father was right about one thing when he said that to me, an 8-year-old boy out hunting with his dad for the first time, ripe-to-bursting for just such a profundity from his generally a-philosophic father: We are part Indian. A genetic cocktail, for sure, and your basic Northeastern non-Blue Blood mix — one that could have resulted from our French Canadian, English, and Algonquian ancestors partying together at some bacchic celebration of the end the French and Indian War.

As for the part about it making a difference, well, that came to be true over time, over the course of the years that followed that watershed day of walking with him and his bow through the crisp, crimson-leafed Vermont woods. But it didn't make a difference in the way one might think — I never became nor have I ever considered myself Native American, at least not with a capital "N." I see the long-term effect of that statement as more like how a microscopic deflection of a spacecraft as it passes the moon might make it miss Mars by a million miles. At midlife, it seems my life missed its orbit around our nice, normal, productive, and profitable early-21st Century American lifestyle; my life was deflected by that simple statement toward a star that is much older, with a gravity field much more ancient than that has captured most folks I know.

My dad rarely brought up our small slice of Indian-ness after that day. The reason for so little elaboration of such a portentous statement,

I believe, is that he didn't really think it was that important. My father never claimed any special cultural connection to Native America because of that trace of blood any more than he claimed to know Parisian culture because we also had a genetic French connection. Aside from a token ration of genes, we weren't in any way Indians and never pretended to be. In fact, as a kid, the closest contact I ever came with an actual Indian was my great-grandfather. He and my great grandmother were the last full-blood Indians in our family, but she had died in a car accident when my father was still a kid. My father's grandfather, though, would pop up every now and then in my childhood, making random, unscheduled visits.

As a kid, on many Sundays, my father and I would drive up to my grandfather's place, a single-wide trailer set in the New Hampshire woods. I would hang out with my father and grandfather as they drank beer and listened to country music on a transistor radio under a big screened-in canopy, unzipping the door only to toss a game of horse-shoes. A couple of times each summer, though, my great-grandfather would show up to join us. "Grandpa runs on 'Indian time'," my dad would explain, meaning there's nothing to explain. I still hold in my mind — the only place a picture remains — the image of this barely five-foot guy with skin the texture of a walnut shell, sitting silently in a cheap lawn chair and smoking rancid cigars. Or wordlessly — he rarely spoke — rising to throw a seemingly endless string of ringers, then returning to his chair and a can of Black Label.

We never saw him in the winter. He disappeared for the cold months, driving alone around the country in a "Mini Winnie," one of those tiny Winnebago campers. He did this until he voluntarily turned in his driver's license at 92 years old, the same year he gave up the cigars.

That's the extent of my "Indian" résumé: a few cryptic statements, an apparition of an old man, and maybe this big Raven beak-like nose of mine. Unless I had $100 in my pocket, that wouldn't even get me into an tribal casino, never mind onto a tribal register somewhere. Nevertheless, we did have a tribe to aspire to, if we had wanted to. My great-grandparents were Abenaki, an Algonquian people once found (actually, getting "found" was when their problems began) from northern New England and the southern Maritimes, down to Cape Cod or so.

But if I were forced to file a form about it with the government, under "tribe of origin" I'd pencil in New England Redneck. I mean "redneck" in its best sense, its operational definition: that uniquely American critter, the blue-collar outdoorsman with the butt-white back and sun-fried head. That was my parents and their cronies: They worked hard during the week, then on their weekends and two-week vacations we were more often than not dragged out fishing, hunting, camping, and walking all over the New England countryside, or out playing sports — softball, hockey, racing motorcycles. The country life. In fact, I grew up thinking country music songs were written specifically about my parents and their friends. Like this verse from Johnny Rodriguez:

Jimmy was a drinking kind of man,
he loved to hear a good hillbilly band.
The scar across his face was Jimmy's brand,
'cause Jimmy was a drinking kind of man.

"He had to have met Jimmy somewhere, maybe in a bar sometime, or fishing or something, but somewhere," my dad would profess whenever that song came on. And I knew what he meant. My father's buddy Jimmy liked to drink, and you couldn't think about him without picturing that gory-yet-venerable scar down his face from where his head had passed, not without some difficulty, through a windshield. To a kid whose heroes were hunters and fishermen, Jimmy was absolutely someone worthy of immortalizing in song.

"Like this new jacket?" Jimmy asked me one opening day of hunting season. We stood on the side of a dirt road somewhere in the backwoods of Vermont gathering gear from the truck in the chilly autumn predawn. This, though, was not just any morning: this was to be the first morning I was allowed to walk into the woods with my own gun. Everything sparkled, everything moved slowly. My arms and legs were heavy.

Jimmy's question broke my trance, some.

He turned left and right, arms raised so I could get a good look at his recent purchase of plaid wool.

"I like it," I said.

"Me too," he agreed, putting down his arms, resting one hand on my shoulder. "Don't ruin it by putting a fucking hole in it."

And there were others, all of them just builders, machinists, mechanics, and sheet-metal workers during the week; and on days off, fishermen, hunters, sportsmen, habitual orienteerers, and natural naturalists. What was called back then "woodsmen." But weekend woodsmen. What are today called Rednecks. For me, though, and for their kids who became my childhood friends, fate and circumstance decreed these men be our guides through our youth and its rites of passage. My father and his buddies had been doing this stuff together since they were kids, and now they were doing it with their kids, passing it on to us. We were Rednecks in training.

My father's role in the tribe was historian. Self-taught, of course. The only tangible product of his studies of New England history was the many, many afternoons, days, weekends, and weeks our family spent driving around Massachusetts, New Hampshire, Vermont, Maine, and New Brunswick in our family's camper. When I was a kid, my personal "Magic School Bus" was a 1967 blue Ford Pickup with an Open Road camper on its back, and Buck Owens or Tom T. Hall or Johnny Cash drawling from an 8-track player. Friday evenings my sister and I would fall asleep in the back and wake up in some other part of New England. For two days we'd traipse around rivers, mountains, marshes, and lakes looking for animals, fish, and whatever else New England was and is. And for something else, something a bit more elusive, but, ultimately, just as important.

We were, as I said, usually fishing or hunting or just walking, but those were also often just an excuse for my father's arm-chair academic agenda: finding — usually with a lot of map interpreting, trial-and-error driving, and backcountry bushwhacking — the places where the Northeast's history took place. These places were so hard to find because my dad generally wasn't concerned with the standard, big events of history. This meant that New England's classic and quaint inns and fishing towns and overgrown post roads and battlefields and townsites were often on our program, but they were just sojourns on the way to our real destination. All of us followed along as my father followed his eyes, searching for his real obsession: the Indians.

Unlike in the Southwest, in the Northeast there is little sign of Native life left. Their organic handiworks were ephemeral in the wet and verdant hills and valleys and seashores of the Northeast. And to ye olde English/nouveau New Englanders, whose priorities were spreading their own divinely sanctioned culture and saving savage souls, the ways of the wayward heathens were not worth preserving. This didn't deter my dad, though. What had been overgrown and reclaimed in terms of dwellings, artifacts, tools, and village sites, what had been killed off in terms of surviving traditions, skills, knowledge, and cultural remnants, what was now buried under pavement and cleared pasture and red-brick and white-clapboard towns, he made up for with educated deduction.

With information from books field-tested with first-hand observation, we drew lines of both reasoning and feeling from what we'd read through what we saw. Continuing on, extrapolating outward (or inward, into our genetic memories, via our inherited intuition) toward what it must have been like to live then and there. Although we never did find a single arrowhead, petroglyph, or rotting wicciup, I nonetheless would leave those trips having seen birchbark canoes running rapids, having eaten lunch in summer fishing villages, having stalked whitetails with a hand-made bow and quiver-full of arrows. I tasted, at least a little, what it must have taken to live there, on that land, off that land.

I couldn't and wouldn't even dare estimate how many Saturdays we spent on these forays into the past with my parents, often accompanied by their gang of like-minded friends and their kids, driving winding black-top or four-wheeling in our two-wheel-drive pickup (I learned to drive by taking the helm of that mud-sunk truck while my dad was out pushing), or walking along languid and redolent rivers and rocky brooks, or orienteering our way through soggy second-growth forests, or climbing forested ridgelines and bald granite monadnocks, all the while striving to perceive the New England landscape as the Indians must have seen it, trying to see it as they would perceive it today.

This was our study, although it, of course, never felt like studying. It was just what we did, it was just what we were doing. It was just fun. It was just a bunch of Redneck weekends. But something insidious was being birthed in all this. The changes were under way: My eyes were being trained to see the land, even under the inevitable festering of highways and towns and subdivisions that spilled across New England in the 1960s and '70s. I was learning how to go native.

Let me make this clear: I don't believe, of course, my parents or their friends had any real plan, blueprint, strategy, educational outline, or guiding vision they were following here. It is only retrospect that I can set all this up neatly and coherently in the lucid terms of hindsight. I wasn't hearing about this whole loopy view I'm today calling "going native." I was doing it. Yet I must say that in this hind-sight view it makes perfect sense that my parents' ramblings around New England would have such a profound impact on me: isn't that what tribes of parents and kids, fathers and sons, mothers and daughters have done for the past million and a half years or so? Not just passing on that day's social skills, but also bestowing on the next generation that deeper knowledge and those timeless experiences that humans living on the land need to survive: skills for self-reliance, awareness of an historical connection with the landscape, kinship with some greater bonded group of people, and the honing of those things in the field through risk, adventure, trial and test.

Now isn't that "native"?

Isn't that *human*?

The dharma (ski) bums

I was lucky enough to catch the caboose of the golden-era run of small Rocky Mountain ski towns. I eddied out for several years in the early 1980s in Winter Park, Colorado, and knew immediately upon arriving I'd passed through some kind of looking glass (located around Berthoud Pass) into a way different culture than the one I'd been comfortably and dutifully plodding through until then.

I was in for a major revelation: I went from making good money in Boston to buying 12 packs of Schaeffer with pocket change, driving a permanently hot-wired '72 Chevy Nova with studded tires (year round, of course), living in a ramshackle and converted 60-year-old post office with three housemates, and again working the jobs that had gotten me through school years before — bus driving, hanging drywall, and prep cooking.

I was very, very happy.

What made this struggling lifestyle into such happiness was the ski-town high society — a mile and a half high. Here, in three towns set at around 9,000 feet in the Fraser Valley, as in many mountain valleys around the West, congregated a group clinging to a small economic niche in the mountains — ski bums, who worked to ski and skied to live. They weren't getting rich, but they were tenacious as lichen on a cliff face. Scruffy as lichen, too — they weren't glamorous, but these were nonetheless the finest, most festive, and least successful — by my old city standards, anyway — people I'd ever met.

What made this society possible was the economically orphaned little towns that made this lifestyle affordable, towns that few people with much money cared much about. Back then, Winter Park Ski Area was still a low-key, little-developed, and family-oriented mountain, not yet aspiring to rise to the status of (yet another) "world-class destination resort." Before my arrival in the Fraser Valley, I'd had no clue this, or places like this, existed, places where people lived because they *wanted* to, even though the financial rewards were ... well, not very rewarding.

Given few opportunities to make much money, and given the Fraser Valley's location in the Front Range's harsh high-altitude environment, the towns were pretty much left to house those willing to put up with those challenges. For most folks, even folks who like to ski, winter in the mountains is fun for a few days or a week; for some, it's even a healthy challenge for five or six months. But there's only a select few willing to endure — and fewer still who find "enduring" a form of "enjoying" — the high-country winter for eight or nine (or ten) months.

And so, with the laws of capitalism functioning quite well, it was affordable for even manual-laboring powder-addicts to live in the Fraser Valley. A ski bum could work to rent or buy a little place, and get their culture socializing on the cheap with their fellow impoverished neighbors. Most importantly, though, they could ski, a lot, and usually for free with ski passes from their jobs, and certainly for free in the surrounding abundance of publicly owned national forest backcountry.

This life is surely not for everyone. This is good. But for some, building a life around having the time to get out; living somewhere where you can get out often, easily, and cheaply; and limiting your financial anchors so you can get out for lengths of time is more important than making money. And if these are your highest aspirations, to live this way for a few years or forever, then, well, where else are you going to live? *How* else are you going to live?

Take, for example, the three ski bums who when I was there were renting an old, small, wood-heated, log-constructed, once-upon-a-time ranch house. With a serious dose of love and $100,000 or so, this old place could make it into one of those glossy "country living" magazines as "rustic." Instead, inhabited by three single males and in need of caulking, a couple boxes of 16-penny nails, roof shingles, six to 10 gallons of paint, and a yard sale, the Morningstar Ranch was merely a boorish fixer-upper. It was perfect.

If I showed up to visit my friends at the Ranch in the morning, I could enter the front door and help myself to a cup of the coffee that always sat rustically — that country-living thing — in a big enamelware coffee pot on the red-hot woodstove. Often Dave would be sitting next to the stove, puffing on a morning pipe and already in his big, heavy, suspendered army-green wool pants. In those days before Gore-Tex and plastic three-pin boots helped make telemarking become as common as telemarketing, these army-surplus trousers were the standard uniform of the tele-marker. In those days, telemarking was a strange, barbaric activity, and telemarkers proudly dressed the part. Once, when I was still an appren-tice telemarker, I crashed into a woman in a floral-print one-piece 100-percent synthetic ski suit that cost more than I was going to make that month. I stood up quickly, spouting apologies, helping up the Southern belle and expecting a scolding. Instead she looked at me with huge, eye-shadowed eyes, and yelled to her husband with Texas-drawled excitement, "Look, honey! A tellurider!"

To be honest, when I first got to Winter Park I didn't downhill ski, although I'd been cross-country skiing in the rolling hills of New England for 10 years or more. The next logical step for me, then, was heavier gear and better turns. So telemarking and I bonded quickly, thanks to the edu-cation rendered by Dave and his housemates, John and Bob. And as a by-product of that education, these guys also ended up serving as role models, helping me earn my wings as another helpless and hopeless Rocky Mountain snow addict.

These guys were good at it. Dave looked like a runaway Scandinavian woodsman, minus the double-bit axe, with a big blond beard and a fishing-tackle tangle of blond hair. He was from New Jersey, but still played the role of the timberman. In the summer he built log homes, at least when he wasn't fishing. Which wasn't often. Myth had it that Dave had spontaneously generated from a pile of decomposing fish guts (a Brown trout, of course) on the grassy bank of Crooked Creek, which was not an impossibility judging by the way he often smelled when we'd meet at the Crooked Creek Saloon on Wednesday nights. (Ah, yes, by gods, the Crooked Creek Saloon! 25-cent drafts from 7 to 8 p.m., affectionately and unofficially referred to in the Fraser Valley as "Wednesday Night at the Fights.") In his defense, though, Dave usually smelled that way because he was such a successful fisherman.

Winter was skiing time, though, and so during ski season Dave drove a snowcat, grooming the mountain until midnight each night while earning a ski pass and seven open a days a week to ski. And that was the point of it all, after all. I was cooking in a Cajun restaurant. Bob, a native New Mexican and expert mountain climber who ended up in the valley because that was where he ran out of money during a cross-country bicycle trip, drove the public buses five nights a week. Trapper John, the jovial trickster in the group, was from Wisconsin, and was by nature, disposition, and skill a Voyageur — an expert canoeist who'd spent a lot of time wandering the Quetico-Superior region of northern Minnesota and southern Ontario. Staying true to the Voyageur spirit, John had become a professional river guide in the summer, hauling tourists for tips rather than furs for trade through the canyons and whitewater of western Colorado. And in the winter, what else? He floated the snow-packed roads in the Fraser Valley in a studded-tired van for a taxi and limo service. And, of course, in the daytime his Voyageur soul explored on skis.

That's what we all did. The physical act of skiing is challenging and engaging enough, sure, but the exploring is what hooked me on this sport of telemarking. True, I also liked that somewhat-outside-the-social-norm feel of being a "pinhead" in a land of alpinists, but what turned me into a zealot was the outside-the-boundaries options unfurled by being good on good backcountry gear. So although we spent a lot days, especially powder days, at the ski area grinding down the bumps and glades and cruisers, more often than not after a couple of warm-up runs we'd take the lift to the top of the area's highest peak, where we'd coyly ski off toward the trees at the top of the westernmost run. Then, out of sight of the lift ops and ski patrol, we'd cut the fence and head west.

Still in potential sight of ski-area gendarmes, we'd scurry with a hurried kick-and-glide across a subalpine pass of low, gnarled, wind-bent firs, and soon dropped into the wide, shallow mouth at the headwaters of a little valley. The upper reaches here were steep and treed, but the drainage downstream deepened and leveled, unwinding gradually toward town, two miles to the north. Out of sight, under the approving and icy stare of that high-altitude diamond-like winter sun, we'd stop for a safety meeting and a snack. Happy as four fat guys at a pig roast, we would just sit there in the snow, relishing the view and savoring the anticipation of the long tear through trees in untracked and knee-deep powder — down the unappreciated and unvisited little valley sequestered just a few hundred yards aside the busy ski area.

Then we'd push off in pairs (always stay in sight of your partner; always know where your partner is) and soar away in tight, bouncing telemark turns, carving each our own S-turn paths down through the trees, laughing and yelping and occasionally pushing ourselves until the snow and slope pushed back. One of us would auger in up to the waist in the sweet white stuff. Up, brush the snow, wipe off my goggles, blow the impacted snow out my nose, and off again.

We couldn't wait to do it the next day. And the day after that. Aside from the occasional crash-and-burn, a telemark turn in untracked Rocky Mountain mid-winter powder is probably — no, definitely — as close as I'll ever get to what I imagine is the ballet dancer's feeling of controlled and confident abandon, that athletic and graceful unleashing of strength. Skiing, though, is better suited to me — not only because I'd look worse than Freddie Mercury in tights and a tutu, but because nothing suits my soul better, I've come to learn, than the exalting abandon of skiing in the mountains, among the trees, along smooth and glistening deep-snow slopes and rolls and ridges and V-valleys.

And once I learned that, I knew I had become a ski bum.

Epilogue: That drainage is today home to several lifts and a hodgepodge of wide, winding blue and green runs. Thousands, sometimes ten thousand, people now wiggle and waggle their way down its designated and groomed runs every day during the ski season. Of course. Things change. Resorts grow. And people grow up: Today the Morningstar Ranch crew are no longer bus or snow cat or taxi-driving ski bums. They've got careers, houses, and wives. Of course.

But ski bumming — that taking of a few years, or several years, or even just one year to live to play and nothing more, to make play the point — changes you, even after you move past ski bumming. Today Dave is a fishing guide living in a fly-in lodge in the Alaskan outback. Bob lives in a house even smaller than Morningstar Ranch, still miles from any town, and teaches at an alternative high school where he takes troubled teens on wilderness adventures to learn about themselves, their abilities and capabilities, and to learn to trust those things. Trapper John, meanwhile, after graduating from a wooden-boat-building school, has moved back within reach of the Boundary Waters region he loves, where he and his wife are certified canoeing instructors.

How about the ski bumming life? In 1983, when I first laid my sleeping bag on a cot in the Winter Park Youth Hostel, the West was in the early phases of a grand and extended economic bust. This is generally considered an undesirable thing, but it is actually an asset if you have little to lose because you have little to begin with, and few material aspirations for the future.

For those with bigger aspirations, though, I guess there ain't enough money in towns full of voluntary poverty. In 1999 Winter Park Resort hired the same designer who brought us the present-day Vail to unleash the full development of the Winter Park base area. Along with that has come to the Fraser Valley the requisite destination-resort amenities from the usual cartel of suppliers: chain restaurants, corporate groceries, the latest destinations of giant resort lodging empires. And more is needed if Winter Park truly aspires to mega-resort status, so the highway to Denver over Berthoud Pass is getting a big-time upgrade, while proposals for a tunnel under the Divide continue to burrow about in the press and real estate offices. And all this progress has, as always, cleared a path for acres and acres of beautiful and enormous second (and third or fourth) houses ("homes" doesn't usually apply to these structures) to blow in like tumbleweeds in a John Ford movie and take root in the woods, in the meadows between the towns, along the many side valleys and ridgelines reaching toward the Divide.

The ski bums are still there, and everywhere there are ski lifts and jobs with passes. They'll always be there. But (and perhaps I say this with that cynical, melancholy voice of the old salt, but I believe this to be true) it ain't what it used to be. Hey, nobody's arguing that capitalism doesn't work. And nobody's arguing about for whom it works. The problem is, nobody's arguing for those it doesn't.

And Morningstar Ranch? It got that big-dollar infusion of loving that turned it into, at last, an expensive, beautiful, valuable restored old ranch house worthy of one of those "country living" magazines.

Natural Bridges

A few years after I became a ski bum who kept forgetting to go home, I sealed my life-changing conversion to the West by going to work in a national park.

Well, a national monument, actually. Natural Bridges National Monument, to be exact, located in southeastern Utah and sequestered away like a desert-junkie's stash between the San Juan River, Canyonlands National Park, Powell Reservoir, and the stunning Abajo Mountains. A small park as national parks go — less than 80,000 acres — and relatively little known, Natural Bridges still has permanent claim to being the first National Park Service unit in Utah. It was created in 1908 by President Teddy Roosevelt himself, who was sickened by the commercial nightmare the private Natural Bridge of Virginia had become (and remains — check it out yourself). The source of Roosevelt's interest was three sandstone spans cut into fins in the meandering walls of White and Armstrong canyons, natural bridges that Roosevelt wanted to stay natural — and national.

By the time I got there nearly 80 years later, it didn't really bother me that I was working in a national monument and not a real national park, because I didn't really "work" while I was there. Not in the common sense of "making money," at least, although physically I labored. The time I was employed there was more of a continuation of my extended vacation from that infamous and always looming Real World of employment. And, kindly, the Park Service supported and nurtured that perspective by not really paying me like a ranger.

But that was okay, because I wasn't really a ranger, anyway. My working holiday with the National Park Service had been arranged through the Student Conservation Association. As a representative of that program, and so visitors wouldn't confuse me with a trained professional ranger (which they did anyway), I was required to wear a brown rather than green uniform, and I wasn't allowed to wear anything that actually said "National Park Service" on it (like maybe I was going to embarrass the U.S. government in the Reagan years?).

I didn't mind, of course, being a Student Conservation Assistant instead of a real ranger, because I wasn't a real student, either.

Unless I counted as a student of life, which, in those care-free, career-free, kid-free and wife-free years of the mid-1980s, I was. And it was this course of study that led me to those three months in this remote outpost of the National Park System. It was a logical stop in the grand tour I was on. Before this sojourn, I had been perfecting my telemark turn and driving a bus for a couple of winters in northern Colorado. And I had spent the previous summer wandering aimlessly across Texas and the Southwest, devouring Edward Abbey's books, filling blank pages with my own mad scribbling, and living out of the back end of a banana-yellow Toyota.

I, of course, didn't plan on always being vagrant and unproductive. While I was randomly poking into the nooks and crannies of the back-country West, in the back of my mind I was still awaiting that moment when I knew it was time to return to the Real World, back to pecking away at my Life's Endeavor — writing The Great American Software Manual — back in Boston.

I, fortunately, never made it back to Boston. Although I can't really nail down when it was on my cross-country walkabout that life-changing decision was made, I believe it was sometime in that time spent at Natural Bridges. In retrospect, I'm not even sure what it was in those three months in that small park that finished off a notion that was growing like a boil on my conscience: the idea that I didn't have to be the

Prodigal Yankee. Regardless of when that moment came, the point is it did come, and since that time I have never resided more than a day's drive from Natural Bridges National Monument.

What did it? It sure wasn't the money, standard of living, or quality of the workplace, things better sought in Boston's red-brick canyons. For the three months I squatted in Utah's redrock canyons, I lived in an official Park Service aluminum trailer and, as I said, I labored: I cleaned toilets, shoveled out fire pits, raked the desert in the campground (being a New Englander I was good at raking), emptied trash cans, talked to visitors in the visitors' center and on the trails, and then picked up after them. Surely these are not worth trading in money and marriage and fresh Boston seafood for.

It might have been the time off. At the end of my five-day work week, I would stuff the Toyota and go, somewhere, out there. Even today when I drive the entrance road to Natural Bridges, I am flooded with the memory of those elated venturing-forths: booming out of the park, my dog hanging out the window and his ears flapping and snapping like hummingbird wings, and Handel's "Water Music" screaming from two tinny speakers. I was going....

And where was I going? Always somewhere new, but always someplace offering the same spirit I found, for example, Easter weekend. That night I found myself on the sheer and vast edge of the southern escarpment of Cedar Mesa, where while I sat there on the rim digesting dinner, I looked up and out over the world before me: The sun set in a red-tide of distant clouds, and as I watched it go down, the full moon rose nearly simultaneously over my left shoulder, crimson and puffing from the effort of the grand celestial see-saw. It soon relaxed into a soft yellow shine, and under that new light I moved right to the final rimrock edge. Twelve-hundred feet below, the canyon of the San Juan was etched out in perfect sinusoidal-wave patterns, the gorge sliding like the river within from a darkening hollow into a translucent, dreamlike, luminescent-blue moon-glow.

That hard world below me drew me to that cliff top all that night, away from huddling around the wind-whipped fire and back to the night-time abyss where in the distance I could see the ghostly spires of Monument Valley. All mine, I felt, daring greediness since my contact with other people was limited to an occasional jet overhead and even rarer car lights clearing a rise thirty miles away.

It wasn't always this thinly settled, though; in fact, more people lived in the Natural Bridges area 800 years ago than do today. I often encountered the remnants of their world, too, and hundreds of their dwellings remain protected in the monument.

Many of these ruins, the inspection of which was also part of my demanding job, were set in dauntingly high, impossibly accessed places, with either chipped "moki" steps or seemingly nothing to reach them. I could not resist reaching and spending time in these places, though, which was sometimes problematic. One time following this impulse, I found myself sliding my belly across a broad, near-vertical slickrock face, desperately clinging to a trail of ancient, worn man-made toe-holds that led like gentle deer imprints to an elaborate set of ruins set deep in a suspended amphitheater. I was determined to reach this place, but already I was fearing the return trip. To reassure myself I tried to imagine the women with babies, and children, and old men and older women who once commuted up and down this wall; hell, if they can do it, surely a well-equipped 20th-century quasi-professional pseudo-student pseudo-ranger will find no trouble....

That helped some, until I reached a vertical band of desert varnish marking where the rare and irregular rain runoff had sanded down the rock face and worn away a six-foot segment of the chipped steps. Problematic.

I looked around for the fire escape, the back door, the servant's entrance, anything that wouldn't require me to turn my body and ascend that not-up-to-code stairway. I found no escape. But while I recounted my various options — exactly one — I also studied the slickrock all around me and discovered the other ever-present sign left by the Ancient Ones: pictographs and petroglyphs carved and painted in seemingly free space, in places and on rock panels with no obvious way for anyone ever having been able to hang there and leave a message. To kill time (before it killed me), I read the usual hieroglyphic spirals and right-angled cornstalks and curly-horned bighorn sheep. I remembered also another pictograph at a nearby, more accessible ruin, a picture dubbed "the strawberry daiquiri panel" since it appeared to be a perfect rocks glass and bent straw. What did they all mean? "Deliveries in rear" ... "Stairway condemned"... "If you lived here, you'd be home now" ...?

Why those people lived in these crazy places I don't know. Nobody really knows. The scientists who study such things say it was a functional response to a dangerous and desperate existence. That's one view. But one thing I noticed as I hung there that day and reflected on my own informal and quite unscientific archaeological surveys is that above all, most ruins offer unique, impressive views. Like what I could see as I slowly twisted around to scale back up from that particular ruin: banded black-and-white-and-red rock walls and pillows and pour-offs decorated and sculpted with dark and light bands and swirls, irregular jagged cuts and fractures and breaks, water stains and wind-polished panels, and hundreds of feet overhead (don't look down....) stood stragglers from another climate zone: daring Douglas firs hiding in shady hollows and nooks of the canyon's upper reaches.

I therefore rebut the experts: I conclude on absolutely no rational or logical ground, but solely on gut sensibility, that surely such a scenic location can not be merely a fortunate byproduct of a strictly tactical decision. The views from Natural Bridges' many former home sites usually seem less like places good for firing arrows from and more like places perfect for.... what? Sipping strawberry — or yucca-fruit — daiquiris, maybe.

These many places I found in my three months around Natural Bridges were amazing things. Wonderful things. But enough to keep me here? To be honest, I don't think it was even these discoveries that made me abandon my late-20th century lifestyle and throw anchor in the sand around here. I could always be a visitor, always make trips to these places. What, then? When I hunt through my journals for a sign of that point of no return, the closest thing to a clue I find is an entry dated somewhere in the middle of my Natural Bridges term. It goes like this:

Sometimes some of us are lucky enough to experience a uniquely marvelous feeling: to realize that at that moment you are exactly where you want to be. Some people strive for that all their lives, but never know it, never reach it, never feel it. To some it never occurs because they're always trying to be where they think they should be.

But some of us have had the good fortune to have felt that realization more than once, although once is enough, for once you've felt it you know what the only thing in life worth trying for is: To always be exactly where we want to be, and to know it.

And some have decided to try to make realizing that the purpose of life: to as often as possible — always if possible — be in the presence of that knowledge that at every moment you are not where you should be, but where you must be.

What makes me think this may be it — that this journal entry may mark that moment — is that I wrote that passage while emptying garbage cans.

But whether that's the moment is irrelevant, for the bottom line remains this: I never went back to the Real World of Boston. But that's okay, because that wasn't really the Real World anyway.

Leaving my sorrows on
the River of Sorrow

$\mathcal{S}$ etting: My dog and I huddle in the back seat of a rattling old Ford Bronco. Moki is curled up on the seat with her head on my lap. I'm drinking my fourth Red Dog while Kansas squeals from the radio. But I'm in a funk even classic rock, cheap beer, and unconditional dog-love can't cut.

Carry on my wayward son....

I'm headed on another river trip, this time down the Rio de Nuestras Senora de los Dolores, the Dolores River. But this isn't starting like most other river trips. Usually the drive to the put in is upbeat and festive, some kind of garrulous pagan festival among whatever fellow river zealots I share my ride with. Today, though, while everyone else gabs and chats, I wallow in sorrow. Not justified sorrow, mind you: I'm whining while headed out on a three-day river trip because I'm headed out on a three-day river trip.

It's true: I float a river of self pity because ahead of me lies three days on one of Colorado's most remote and majestic high-country canyon rivers, one of our backyard gems, and at high-water, no less ... Yet I fret over how much work I'm leaving at home, so many duties and chores I can't get done because I'm going on this river trip. These waves of work-and-money insanity are the nature of life here on the West Slope of

Colorado, sometimes — at least the lifestyle that is built around piecing together enough part-time work to leave lots of chunks of time to wander around out there. The lifestyle I chose. Sometimes, though, I find I sink into the troughs of those waves and lose the bigger West Slope perspective. Like now. Like the past few days

By 9 a.m. the next morning, we're on the water. Moki and I push off onto the chilly and swollen late-spring flow behind the other two boats. A few strokes point us downstream, to the west. Ahead, cumuli nimbi rise like beehive hairdos somewhere over Utah, the Beehive State, meteorological gateway to Colorado.

Launching from Bradfield Bridge dumps us into Ponderosa Gorge, one of the stranger and more dramatic places I've floated. Here, a rocky stretch of Class II water meanders through the up-side of the Dolores Anticline. With each mile the canyon's walls deepen, with no hint of the piñon-juniper forest and irrigated bean fields along its rim. The most beguiling part of the float for me, though, is the ponderosas themselves. Sprouting along the floor of the rocky gorge is a ribbon of these old-growth giants, deepening the feeling of isolation from the semi-arid world above. This riverine grove grew from pine cones washed down from the cooler high country upstream, and in the canyon they create a topsy-turvey biotic shift, with this ponderosa forest standing at a lower elevation than the piñon-juniper landscape on the mesa top above.

Moki and I drift alone, the other boats somewhere up around the gorge's tight bends. Above us steep cliff-sides fall to fans of rubble strewn with great, discarded blocks of former cliff face. On the canyonsides, scrub oak and piñons grab whatever rootholds they can secure — more straggling West Slope strugglers. Whistles of birds pierce the whisper of the river. Moki stands on the bow peering and sniffing into the cool of the mid-spring upstream breeze, her nose twitching busily, threatening to drag her on lines of scent right off the boat. I lean back on the rowing frame, sipping a beer, buck-naked and prostrate, as passively receptive as a solar panel. And once again, like so many times before, I find the river debugging my bugged-out attitude, as the static of the rational is displaced by the soothing of the sensuous.

The River. Any river. Every river. If the West Slope's landscape and people kept me loitering across the Divide longer than planned when I first arrived for a ski-bumming sojourn fifteen years ago, then river running snared me for good. The first river trip I ever took launched when a girlfriend and I were "between jobs," deliberately. We were spending a spring and summer in the early '8os driving around the Southwest and living out of the back of her car on the crumbs of our ski-season money. We were passing through Moab (then still a frontier town of desert rats, river runners, light tourism prospectors, and hard-rock miners) in early May, before the Colorado River rises to greet jonesing river guides like a vein (or bag?) of gold.

One morning we found some people hanging around the office of a river company, hung over and drinking coffee, and we offered to clean and organize their warehouse in exchange for a river trip. Two days of manual labor — that portentous first time getting to fondle river gear — got us a day on the river. And got me yet another of those seemingly innocuous events after which you suddenly find yourself following some new karmic compass bearing. You can't plan epiphanies.

Our first trip was down the Colorado, putting in twenty miles upstream of Moab then floating back down to town. It was one of the company's training trips, and our guide for the day was training to be the barge rower, the standard entry-level position in the river-guide community. A side of beef wearing an open flannel shirt with the sleeves cut off and an "Alta" ballcap, he looked like he would've been at home in a pickup with a throaty snarl and a confederate flag in the rear window. He had the rough and rugged truck, but no flag — instead he had a "Hayduke Lives!" bumper sticker and a patchwork of duct tape stitching together the rear window.

Still, the redneck rocker tag was supported by the quality of the ride to the put-in. We hurtled out of the fertile little Moab Valley and turned right, into the redrock corridor of the Colorado River. While we flew along that wild ribbon of pavement, following its weaving around K-Mart-sized sandstone boulders flung from the cliffs above, our guide just grinned and yacked about skiing and line-cooking and construction jobs and river trips, all the while puffing on a big bambu he kept trying to hand us. In the pauses in his talking, he turned up the ZZ Top:

Thhhhhhhat's right....

When we finally fishtailed into the put-in and stumbled from the cab, our driver transformed. Over the next several hours, from under that hill-billy garb emerged some kind of pagan pilgrim, and we could see him consummating his faith and reverence with his first day soloing on the river. It was like witnessing the enlightenment of some bubba Buddha, like seeing the live birth of a river rat right before our eyes.

Then it happened to me, too. That one day sliding down Professor Valley was all I needed; the next spring I, too, was training as a river guide up in the Colorado high country, learning to read current and rocks, practicing rescuing wrapped boats and bobbing swimmers, surviving my own flips and involuntary swims. And that's how I spent the next dozen summers, living out of a tent, traveling between rivers and taking people out, out there, damn near every day from May to September.

Now almost two decades later, I find myself married to a fellow (former) whitewater guide. We own our own boat, and we use it, a lot. Now though, our trips are mostly flat-water family ventures. Getting our kids on the river is the primary drive in our lives now, and one of the main reasons my wife works in the schools and I cobble together that sometimes mind-blinding and spirit-gnawing series of part-time occupations. The resultant and inherent perpetually fluctuating cash flow is, of course, worth that river time. I just forget that sometimes. Until the river reminds me.

The next morning, worries return — but this time it's not over bills and work.

John and I rig our boats in the flat but warm morning light. We won't be leaving for a while, and everyone else drinks coffee, standing around trying to absorb the sun, and chattering about the upcoming day's big events. But preparing to leave isn't really the point here — John and I are just savoring the sensuous foreplay that is rigging a boat.

While I'm strapping dry boxes and clamping down dry bags, though, something gnaws at my gut. It's not the coffee, I realize, as I'm careful to strap in each piece of gear with that extra strap that gets that extra yank reserved for big water days.

This will be a big water day.

At the canyon's deepest point, 2,300 feet, near the town of Dove Creek's water pumping plant, the Dolores starts down the backside of the Dolores Anticline. You can see this in the changes: The terrain suddenly transforms into Utah-esque desert canyon. The river quickens. Class II and III rapids start appearing around corners. The most undeniable and unavoidable change, though, comes eight miles downstream from the pumphouse, at Snaggletooth Rapid, the most challenging rapid on the entire Dolores River: a football-field-long, Class IV-V (depending on flow) run around rocks, over low falls, and through unavoidable holes. I've run Snag a few times before, including at this high water level, and have always been successful. I also know that means nothing when the water's sucking you downstream into the maw once more.

This much is clear: I love running rivers. And I've put the time in to get pretty good at it. But rapids still rattle my guts. Thinking about rapids still rattles my guts. This is probably because I've seen what they can do — because I've experienced what they can do. That dull gnawing in my stomach this morning feels an awful lot like the lingering psychological bruise from banging my head on the bottom of a raft stuck surfing the same hole I, myself, was circulating in. It feels like that sinking feeling of watching the bow my boat eclipse the sun, and then continue on its over-head trajectory toward becoming the stern. It feels like dozens of times

I've found myself suddenly gasping short, erratic breaths while bobbing in frigid but furious whitewater.

Yet here I am, again. And again the question must be asked (maybe it's my duty to my mother, eh?): Why trade the worry and risk of getting submerged in the day-to-day business world for this, the risk and worry of submersion in a thrashing rapid? A damn fine question, as always. And it's hard to explain to those who haven't been there, because the best explanation is more of a physical feeling than a rational reasoning. It's a yin-yang thing — a dance of forthright fright and addictive adrenaline that restores some valid and valuable sense of the middle, something the dance of income/expense or work-week/weekend time doesn't come close to matching. Most importantly, perhaps, is that facing a stretch of whitewater requires a perspective — again, more a sensibility than a rationale — that continues to enlighten and enliven that more mentally demanding day-to-day life long after the river time is over. For me, anyway. For some of us, anyway.

And some of us need hits of that: the restorative medicine of the river that is addictive and indispensable for us river rats. Still, it's a little bit different for me these days. Since having kids, it seems the yin of restraint has been outweighing the yang of risk, which used to rule. I still don't mind betting on my skills, but with kids in the picture the wagers have undeniably escalated. Maybe it's partly a symptom of middle age, as well, but these days I'm pretty content just floating along and gawking at the pretty scenery.

But somewhere inside I sense this: I owe the river its whitewater, at least occasionally.

Back on the river, we drift farther into the heart of Colorado's West Slope. The river enters a shallow rock-walled gorge, 20 to 30 feet high, within the grander canyon. Ponderosas peer down on me from the benches above, a stark and dark red-on-green in a thickly-banded slot in the earth. The canyon's dull glare feels like a steely stare as we wind farther downriver. Or maybe it's those dark, glowering clouds that imbues the atmosphere with that ominous air. Or maybe it's simpler than that: just the 40-degree air temperature, only a few degrees warmer than the water temperature. Or maybe I'm just paranoid.

Either way, inevitably and unavoidably, in the early afternoon we approach Snag under the oppressive weight of a low, thick sky. The river seems to pick up on my anxiety: As we pull up to the scouting trail, thunder rumbles up the canyon on a fierce wind, and an icy rain pelts us. The roar of the rapid taunts from around the next bend.

A rock outcropping offers us a look at our challenge: Three big holes, the third with a raft-flipping wave, then a maze of clawing rocks; then Snaggletooth rock itself, a black serrated fang the size of an upended Suburban sawing through the main current. It's a hundred yards of froth and force, of the unending Zen-like flow of determined water breaking on unyielding rock.

It looks even worse than I remember it, and I remember it bad enough. I suggest to my companions that we abandon our boats and gear, scale the gorge, and take up bowling. But then we study the rapid for a while. Slowly a route appears and we devise a plan. Then we discuss options should the river have other plans. Any river guide can look good on a clean run through whitewater, but the quality of river runners is measured by how poised they remain facing the unexpected events that unfold in the pumping heart of a rapid.

We could study this forever, but poise can't be planned. At some point you just have to row. I tie Moki to a tree at the bottom of the rapid, John and I slap each other's shoulders, someone unleashes a lunatic howl, and we go....

My stomach shuts up once I make my first stiff strokes toward the lip of the drop. No use worrying anymore; in here, only actions matter. So I act: I push to punch the three big holes, skirt the curling maw of the flipper-wave, then thread the rock minefield. But I have a closer encounter than planned with Snaggletooth. The surging river throws me so near the tooth I could reach out and slice cheese on its razor face, but I manage to dodge the fang by going with the flow of the river, spinning my big boat around the edge, and diving into the roaring pit of crashing water behind the rock.

The boat and I bob back up, dripping but upright. I throw a fist in the air and yelp and laugh. Then I crank the oars toward shore to free Moki and watch my friends weave their way through the whitewater.

Later, we stand around at the bottom of the rapid high-fiving and beaming. Then I move off alone, squat by the river, point my face into the cold mountain rain and savor its earthy erotica. It's frigid and stinging, but not unpleasant. It is what it is. I glance back up at Snaggletooth. It's nasty, scary, and dangerous, but not right or wrong, good or bad; it is just what it is. I'll get rattled the next time I row up to it again, but I will row it again. I want to.

That's what the river reminds me: Life is Class V sometimes, so shut up and row. Stay poised. Enjoy what it is.

And that is the exact opposite of whining.

Back to the Future 4(Corners)

*I*t was bound to happen. Tempt fate as many times as I have with as many crossings of Wolf Creek Pass as I've made this summer (and the past few summers, and the next several to come), and it was inevitable. Stopped by a flagger for the pass's endless construction, I would sit out there on the embankment above the South Fork of the Rio Grande, listening to the hypnotic slosh of the whitewater, with that high-altitude sun like a heavy blanket over my driving-tired shoulders. Do that enough times and I figured I would fall asleep sometime.

One afternoon I did, right there on the rocks on the side of the highway.

The problem was, when I woke up, the highway was empty. The line of silent cars queued up behind the chubby flagger in the orange vest was gone. My first question was why my wife and kids might have driven off without me — I figured they'd had a bellyful of my bellyaching about all this tax-funded road work that was destroying a lovely and functional mountain road, so even more 48-foot RVs pulling Jeep Wagoneers can slog just as slowly as ever over the mountains but without any of the annoying bends in the road.

I could see how they could grow weary of my griping. But at that point it didn't matter, since I was out there on the side of the highway still an hour and a half or so from home (if I had a car, which I didn't). But I figured a fresh queue of backed-up traffic would be forming soon, so all I would have to do would be to get someone to believe that I'm not dangerous even though my family abandoned me asleep by the side of the road. So I waited, for what seemed like a long time. But then again, the day had taken on a surreal sort of glow, so I wasn't really sure.

When finally a vehicle came winding up around the bend, I stuck my thumb out, and the pickup pulled to a stop next to me. It was a new-looking rig, at least in model; cosmetically, though, it looked like it might've been sitting in a wash outside of Bluff, Utah, for the last couple of decades. The only fresh paint was on the door, where was printed "Raven Adventures." The door screeched and sank toward the road a few inches when I pulled it open. After I climbed in, it took two hands and three tries to yank it back into place.

My rescuer was a Nordic looking guy about my age, sporting an unbuttoned flannel shirt. Flyaway blond hair leapt from under a greasy ball cap, and his big grin seemed to hang from his bushy moustache.

"Trapper John," he announced cheerily as we shook hands. Then his hand flashed to catch the glovebox that had popped opened when the truck banged through what felt like a giant pothole.

"Latch's broken," he apologized, as he put his hand back on the wheel just in time to swerve sharply to avoid a small boulder in the road. "Hard to find that part anymore."

I heard him, but my attention had been grabbed by the road. It was a mess. It looked like it hadn't seen roadwork in a generation, never mind being in the midst of a massive pork-barrel "improvement" project. In fact, the lofty and lovely cliff face I'd been watching get disassembled all summer, the dynamiting of which was causing the endless hours of stalled traffic, was already back a good 150 feet from where I'd seen it last. The pavement, though, looked well on the way to returning to being a dirt road.

If only all highway construction could be so de-constructive, I thought wistfully. Trapper John, meanwhile, was still rapping proudly about his truck.

"... an '03, with original interior and paint. Well, the paint's kinda' fried. Of course the engine had to go — still ran on real gas, and I can't afford that shit, even if I could find it — but the motor has a sound chip. Wanna' hear what it sounds like with a 405 and straight pipes?"

He typed something into a keypad where the ash tray should be, and a throaty roar began grumbling from under the bed of the truck.

"These were real machines," Trapper John said thoughtfully to the windshield, as he studied the road ahead. We had crossed the Divide and were approaching the big switchback that offered a big turnout with a view over the San Juan Valley. But the overlook was gone. In fact, most of the road was gone, apparently fallen away into the valley below, leaving only a one-lane-wide section clinging to the mountainside. Trapper John was riding the brakes while the engine imitated the sound of downshifting. "... Do it all the time," he was saying to himself, "... just gotta' ease her around ...."

This probably would've been more disturbing if I wasn't hypnotized by the view: A whole town — a sizeable gleaming city, even — filled the once-majestic Upper San Juan Valley like a bowl of old oatmeal. Rows of palatial houses hung from hillsides in the distance, where just a few days ago (right?) stood the unbroken green of the San Juan National Forest. Across the valley floor pulsed roadways that also weren't there when I drove up the valley less than a week before.

"Pagosa?" I asked, pointing dumbly out the window.

"Well, DisneyTimeWarnerToyotaMobilWalMartFairfield at Pagosa Resort, yeah."

The view slipped away behind us as we tight-roped the ledge and began rolling down the rough grade again, skirting potholes, negotiating slumped-away sections of roadway, and threading boulders strewn like litter.

"I could pick up the interstate from Taos to Durango," Trapper John was saying now, "but I just love these old roads. There are lots of them down in the SacZone, if you don't mind sneaking in."

"Sac ... ?" I asked, just one of innumerable questions swelling in my head. "I'm, um, not from around here... I mean, I thought I was, but ...," I babbled weakly.

He grinned at me again. "Yeah, the National Sacrifice Zone. It's against the law — what isn't, eh? — but I don't mind sneaking in. Hard to guard the whole thing, so they try to scare people away, saying that all that crap they buried in those big spent coal mines along the New Mexico border and pumped into the dried-up gas wells everywhere could be toxic for thousands of years. I mean, even the Utes took all the money they made selling their land so the country could dump all that non-degradable plastic they'd been making for a hundred years and bought themselves an island in the Caribbean. Opened up their own country."

I was starting to crave a beer.

"Well, anyways, sneaking into the SacZone is the only place you can go any more without paying for a permit or turning in a friggin' itinerary just so you can be surrounded by a thousand other campers. Even the Wilderness Areas are fucked since they started letting personal aircraft in. They make those things now so any moron can use one without auguring into a mountainside, as God meant flying morons to do."

His timing was impeccable: Trapper John handed me a beer from the truck's center console. The familiar Budweiser label was stamped in the middle of the can, which felt like plastic. Across the top was printed: "100% Organic Hemp Cellophane Can!" I copied Trapper John as he peeled the tab off the top and ate it, washing it down with a long sip.

"I swear the can's stronger than the brew," he laughed, pushing his hat back on his head. He then yanked the wheel around a refrigerator-sized block of sandstone.

"Think about it," he spouted on, eyes starting to bulge like some kind of redneck preacher, or one of my Earth First! friends at 1 a.m. in the El Rancho Tavern. "My grandparents were able to just hike, hunt, fish, ride a bike or a horse, or go camping all over this place, anytime, for free. It was almost all public land then, and not many people. There were no big highways or airports for hundreds of miles."

He looked back to the road. "It must've been great."

My head hit the dashboard as we skidded to a stop. We were down by the last switchback, which was blocked by a fresh deadfall Lodgepole pine that lay across the four-wheel-drive road that was once Wolf Creek Pass. For the next half hour, we pulled the tree to the side of the road with a chain and Trapper John's restored 2003 Ford F250 "classic." Then we sat on the tailgate and talked, sharing a bag of salted roasted dung beetles (barbeque flavor) and drinking Budweisers from edible cans that he said were left over from the guiding trip he'd just finished.

Trapper John, I learned, was Raven Adventures — "A throwback to the small-time outfitters," he proclaimed. "Fortunately the government has to give a few token outfitting permits to locally owned, non-corporate companies," he told me. "But there aren't many of those anymore." Those days ended, he said, with the passage of the "Public Lands and Rivers Final Resolution Act," 50 years ago, which, he explained, divvied up the public lands once and for all between states, corporations, and the federal government. The undeveloped country that's left, he said, is so carefully rationed and managed for profit that if you don't have friends or very good luck to help you score a permit, then you'd better own your own ranch, game farm, or fishing stream.

Seems my enterprising friend found his own niche, though: he became a "privateer." He defined this occupation as he said it was outlined in the federal property-rights statutes that outlawed the practice: "Privateering is profiting from leading paying customers onto or across private land, public lands, or allocated rivers without having paid fees or acquiring proper permitting."

"Fu' tha'," Trapper John mumbled, his mouth full of his fifth can. He swallowed, and followed it with a gulp. "You ask me, the land, all land, is a birthright. And that's the attitude I help people experience who aren't rich enough to own or visit wild land. I open the land back up to them, and I'm affordable. Of course, it's against the law. But these folks have a kickass time, the rush of their lives, especially if we have to run and ditch. Usually, though, we just sneak around, poach the views, snag some fish or small game. Big game are usually all tagged with beacons and alarms, of course, since they're the money makers. Business is good for me, though. Lots of return business."

I'll drink to that, I thought, as I grabbed another can of cold plastic. I was thinking I might have a job, too, should I find I couldn't get back to my early 21st century life.

Trapper John was on a roll by now as he opened another can with his teeth. He tore off the tab and tossed it to a fat black raven staring at us intently from the top of the fallen tree trunk. The raven picked it up, look at us again like offering a thanks, then flapped away over the cliff edge.

"That's what the 'raven' in 'Raven Adventures' means. I've decided to live like a raven rather than a cow. Think about ravens: even though they thrived during the last ice age, they're still thriving everywhere on earth. And they're still wild, even though they have had to adapt to this land, now, just as it is — they, too, have to live in this technological ice age we created. Ravens thrive by staying wild where they are, in the circumstances they're in. Most people, though, are domesticated, just so many more cows, doing what they're told, following the fences penning them in, satisfied with the salt-licks they're given.

"I offer raven-style trips."

The first real quiet moment since I got in Trapper John's truck followed then, while we watched the sun set over rows of hundreds of stucco California-style cliff-side houses lining the San Juan Valley. And that's when I heard the rumbling. First it was like one deep grumble, then more and more bass voices joined in. When I looked up I could see the avalanche had already grown into a roaring wall of rolling rock ripping our way. As we dove to the ground the last thing I felt was my beer spilling across my cheek....

.... As my dog's tongue lapped my face again, and I jolted upright. Dozens of car engines were already revving, sounding relieved to be finally back at work, at last given permission to roll on up the pass again.

"Let's go!" my wife called from the end of the dog's leash. "Hey, were you asleep?"

Cortez: the real Wild West

I was driving west (always west!) with a friend recently, when we pulled into the sprawling tidewater debris line of greater metro Cortez, Colorado. You know, the standard American bland-named, economy-sucking, parking-lot-moated colonial outposts of well-known fast-food shacks, sweat-shop department stores, and chain video-rental places. This strip of highway could be leading you anywhere in the modern West — Bolder, Longmall, Santa Fake, Flagstuff, Sodoma, Bland Junction.

Once we got through this dead zone, we slid into the heart of downtown. We pooled up behind a red light, idling there alongside the pickups and rusty '72 Chevy Novas and low riders and horseshit-covered duelly-wheeled diesel pickups and growling one-eyed rez cars that prowl Cortez on a Friday night.

I could see my friend grow a dark look, like a five-o'clock shadow. "Cortez," he sneered, glaring out the passenger window.

"Cortez!" I cheered, staring out the driver-side window.

Yippee for Cortez! My favorite town in the Four Corners! Where some see unsightly, irrational, real-estate devaluing anti-urban blight, I see untamed human wildness.

I just love it all: The unrestricted, unpermitted, unmanaged, un-land-use planned, covenant-free (as it should be!) and thoroughly pragmatic (function is beauty!) disarray of adobe and "manufactured," asbestos-sided and sunburnt-paint-peeling houses that circle downtown

20 blocks deep, more like a semi-permanent encampment than any kind of carefully constructed urban environment. And these eclectic neighborhoods are further spiced with winding trash-filled arroyos, snaking canals, and random stands of sage and rabbitbrush.

Lying at the core of these layers is downtown Cortez. On the surface, the town may seem slow and sickly. But if you look deeper — like, get out of your car and walk around — you begin to see the real secret of Cortez: It's still alive. It's still wild.

Granted, it may not be a pulse any resort-coveting empire-building tourist-pimping Chamber of Commerce will detect — or appreciate. But regardless, if you look closely — no, if you feel closely — you can hear it, smell it: there's something still breathing in Cortez. And it's refusing to let all its blood be sucked by the corporate leaches, even as they hang limply on the skin of the city. Like a hogan sitting arrogantly in front of the rectangular government-issued pre-fab house on a reservation backroad, local business illogically persists in Cortez.

Which is why in Cortez they laugh at the more "successful" towns, like nearby Durango, Moab, or Telluride: because downtown Cortez is still a lichen-tough hold out of hard-scrabble, sole-proprietor, neighbor-known enterprises that haven't yet surrendered to yet another row of humiliating tourist trappers. Imagine! A Main Street of thrift stores and greasy-spoon cafés and little bookstores, and even a used-paperback store and movie house and coffee-and-burrito-serving Airstream trailer that sits staring at Mesa Verde while its rounded chrome finish echoes the morning sun.

Imagine! A town that hasn't yet become another brothel of a tourist attraction, with the accompanying socialized costs of supporting a tourist industry that "resort" towns suffer: overpriced costs of living, ridiculous real estate prices, a manufactured theme-park identity, painful traffic, silly tourist hordes, endless t-shirt shops, and the inevitable influx of both wealthy residents (and their needed supporting infrastructure of expensive eateries and dainty coffee shops and knickknack shacks) and migratory roughneck construction crews — and the flood of all their kids into the schools that these second-home and short-term sojourners inevitably refuse to support.

Cortez is none of that. Cortez just is.

And not much of the American West today just is.

This is too much of the American West today:

Not too long ago I found myself driving through Salt Lake City. The Mormon Mecca today, of course, is all highways and home-building and Home Depots and bitter drivers swarming in swirling traffic — and growing like a melanoma thanks to jet-commuters from L.A. and the 2002 Winter Olympics. I remember an image as we drove from the city itself into the foothills: an awkward stand of trophy homes, garish and tacky and trying much too hard to look much too big, crammed together like tenements (but not as beautiful as brownstones), all clinging to a few steep narrow benches of broken rock and scrub oak at the foot of the Wasatch, with great (and pricey) views west toward the fishing-tackle tangle of highways and some brown-haze-obscured distant peaks.

Nouveau-riche heaven. A realtor's wet dream. The early 21st-Century West in a nutshell.

On this trip to Utah, though, I was staying above and away from all this. I was in Alta, high in the Wasatch Ranch, there on a ski trip with my wife's family. On one of those days, rather than skiing with everyone else in the group, I opted to take the day to stay in the condo and write. We were lodged in one of those expensive ski-town rent-a-condos built with the care of a Happy Meal box that have spread like athlete's foot across Rocky Mountain ski towns. Settled in that setting, I found that rather than writing I was just staring at the condo's walls. They were adorned with a smattering of tin Kokopelli cutouts (of course tastefully minus the proud free-swinging members true Kokopelli petroglyphs display) and romantic paintings of Indians on horseback in misty, pastelly wilderness settings.

I wondered what the owner of this townhome (who lived in a city far, far away) really thought about The People today, if at all. No matter anymore, though, eh? These were safe, soft images of The Vanished Vanquished Ones. Of course, those who think the Indians are dead haven't been to a powwow. Those who think the Indians lost haven't been to a tribal casino. It's true: The Home Team always bats last.

Well, needless to say, with these nagging thoughts in my head, no writing was getting done. So I loaded a daypack and headed down the road for a walk.

Alta is a smattering of Alp-ish buildings, a business district of steep-roofed buildings that give it the look of a mining town — mining skiers' billfolds — huddled on the side of a steep valley and standing in stark cultural contrast to the more-recent condominium shantytown. But it's the valley that kept drawing my attention.

Ah, the valley! Radically vertical sides, ragged limestone ledges and bluffs, snow and evergreens clinging where possible, and sometimes where impossible, rising up to bare summit-crags floating in the thin-aired blue. Those razorback ridges and knife-point summits throw rocky runouts from every crevasse and couloir; and these avalanche chutes ignore the imposition of the roadway laid up the valley bottom, crossing it from each side like stitches closing a wound. Sometimes in the winter here, avalanches cover parking lots and close access to the canyon for a week at a time. Wildness lives!

I walked where there are no sidewalks — resort designers don't expect people on a ski vacation to walk. I wandered downvalley a mile or so to the ritzier Snowbird resort. My plan (as much as I ever have a plan) was to sneak into an fancy spa and weight room at some expensive hotel complex. I didn't plan well: I chose to forego the name-brand camouflage and instead sauntered about arrogantly in full eco-scorn, torn jeans over long underwear and an annoying environmental t-shirt.

Still, I waved to the desk attendant at the first high-rise I got to, took the elevator up to the 9th floor to the glassy health club, and entered a high-tech "fitness center" where a half-dozen well-fed women in incandescent Lycra pounded on walking machines. (And why not get out and ... walk? Maybe because there are no sidewalks?) They stared vacantly at

CNN on a half-dozen TVs as I walked past the seven-foot-high tinted-glass walls overlooking the valley floor — although no one was looking that way — and changed in the bathroom.

And so ended a decade-long pilgrimage. When I first moved West in the early '80s, during the entire epic blaze out from the East Coast the friend I came with regaled me with a steady stream of stories of ski bumming in Alta in the '70s. People were wild there, he said. They lived, rather than made a living. I was a neophyte, and these came as reports from the underground, tales of power from a world I'd never known or even knew existed. Already, though, I was free-falling in the rush to be part of it. For a while, anyway — until I returned to resume my regularly scheduled programming once I "got it out of my system."

That particular plan failed when I realized that "it" was my system.

I found my personal bit of the Golden Days of the Ski Bums in northern Colorado, and it took me more than 10 years — until this trip — to finally make it to Alta to see what my friend had been talking about. And as I worked out in that hotel in Snowbird, I realized I wasn't seeing it, and never would, here anyway. This wasn't where when my friend had ski bummed. And I understood then, again, that another chunk of my habitat had been devoured before I even got there.

And I don't see it getting better. Here's why:

Later that spring, I was at a regional business forum on growth. I was there to deliver one of my standard rants on the need to keep our public land public (and other unreasonable demands); others were there to talk about the threats to wildlife of trophy-ranchette development, the inevitability of the Big Fire thanks to our county's build-whatever-as-long-as-you-have-money form of so-called planning (our region is historically a fire-ecology environment), and how our lack of planning is also sucking us into a highway hellhole. The usual stuff.

During the question-and-answer time after my harangue, a realtor and I exchanged some enjoyable and pointed barbs. I think we were bantering about whether or not growth really is inevitable — I was thoughtfully outlining my modest proposal of returning the region's highways to dirt to deter the half-hearted — when I posited the obvious question: When does it end?

The realtor had thought about this, it appeared. "It doesn't," she said blankly. Then she smiled and assuredly gave The Rap: "We need to keep growing so we'll have better jobs and more income."

But — somebody else in the audience joined in — what'll it be like even if we have more money, but with twice as many people living here?

She looked a little thrown by this one, but recovered quickly. "Well, we'll have to learn to live among more people, like the Japanese do. We'll enjoy small spaces and follow a code of respect for how to treat people in crowds."

I swear she said this.

Of course she said this. She's right, of course. Alta is all of us, all the West. Or it will be soon.

But ... as long as there are something left, there's hope — Remember: the home team always bats last. And I find hope in the West's remaining remnant independent towns, like Cortez. So when that kind of stuff starts to get me down, I head west (always west!), and I remember where the real Wild West still is, what it is, and who inhabits it. I know where Kokopelli hasn't been castrated.

Wild People, Unite!

This is what you do:
Love the earth and sun and the animals,
despise riches,
give alms to everyone that asks,
stand up for the stupid and crazy,
devote your income and labor to others,
hate tyrants,
argue not concerning God,
have patience and indulgence toward the people,
take off your hat to nothing
known or unknown
or to any number of men,
go freely with powerful uneducated persons
and with the young
and with the mothers of families,
read these leaves in the open air
of every season of every year of your life,
re-examine all you have been told
at school or church or in any book,
dismiss whatever insults your own soul,
and your very flesh shall be
a great poem.

— Walt Whitman

Wild people, unite!

$\mathcal{S}$ aturday morning, we drive west. We roll over the south flank of the La Platas, cruise underneath the north wall of Mesa Verde, then circle around the top of the Sleeping Ute Mountain's war bonnet and into McElmo Canyon. Here we enter "No National Monument." Or so the hand-painted signs in many yards say. It seems like a much better name than the tedious and wordy Canyons of the Ancients National Monument the government recently assigned the region.

Onto Dinetah's oil-and-gas badlands, where I tell Mark, my traveling companion on this adventure, the story of another time a friend and I were blazing down this same road. We approached a small, rect-angular, pre-fab plywood government home — the anti-hogan — set in the dusty brown chaparral, where stood a small maze of bombed-out household appliances around which played two kids. As we approached my friend lifted his hand in greeting from his open window. The kids looked at us. Then the oldest returned a single-digit editorial on our kinship.

As we passed we watched them hug and laugh hysterically, like ... well, like kids. My friend and I turned up the Allman Brothers and roared on, laughing quite happily ourselves.

Onward. We drive past cow-burnt sandhills, past tireless pumpjacks, past wind-swept trailersites and trash-filled arroyos. Fueled by coffee, the latest war news, the dust-bowl views, and the anticipation of getting to the wilderness, Mark and I share angry talk — it's part of the therapy this trip offers — about the fact we're down to the stems and seeds of wilderness here in the 21st century. I rant about how my kids need wilderness; Mark rails back about how we've got to fight for it. Mark fights. He's an angry young man, and that's why I like him. Actually, he's an angry middle-ager afflicted with the suicidal tendency to say what he thinks, like me, but I like him anyway.

And that's why I like the "No National Monument" signs. That's why I delight in those kids who flipped us off. When it comes to earning my respect and admiration, it matters less to me what someone's particular argument is as it does that he or she argues at all. I'm happy to argue; society should be messy. I believe on some level way deeper and more fundamental than thinking that the hope of our species lies not any particular platform or plan, but in the survival of raw wildness. Not just wilderness, but human wildness.

If that's a formula for chaos, so be it. If science has shown anything it's that chaos and diversity are the engines of evolution. (Someone please tell this to the government, the genetic engineers, and the religious right, okay?) Where there's chaos, there's wildness, and wildness is my faith. In my disturbed logic, then, where there's someone lifting a finger, there's hope.

We are headed somewhere along the San Juan River. This destination was my idea; I needed to come here. I need the river, that entrenched thread weaving together the cryptic spires of Monument Valley, the forbidding escarpment of Cedar Mesa, the snow-cloaked slopes of the Abajos, and the temporarily submerged depths of Glen Canyon. My personal heartland. There are stories here, and since it's February, always the longest short month of the year, my spirit and body need a hit of those stories. Even though I've been out here only some 20 years, just half my life, this place has become my Place.

Another one of my peculiar perspectives: We need land to survive, yes; but more than that, for health we require Place: land that is mean-ingful. I don't mean this as some mystical woo woo: this is human psychology, evolved biology. Think about the people who truly lived in these canyons for hundreds of generations, for longer than even they themselves could remember. To those people, the landmarks that com-prise this place weren't novelties visited on weekends or vacations; for true natives, each canyon pool, amphitheater overhang, natural arch or bridge, or scenic vista were neighborhood sights that they were born under, walked past, climbed over, mulled on, worked by, and gathered food near every day, as their ancestors had forever. They knew they'd die surrounded by these landmarks.

What stories this place must have told then! Every wrinkle in the land would have a tale invested in it, stored in it. Eventually, the people's history would be remembered by the Place. Not an "accurate" academic history, but a true history — stories shaped and reshaped by each gener-ation, each teller, each telling, evolved and honed not to the sharpest accuracy but to the most vital meaning, earning their tenure among the people by offering morals, lessons learned by the people and worth remembering, worth passing on. Stories about who they are.

In a hunter-gatherer's world, the land was the culture. The physical place was inherently interwoven with the people's identity and character. It was all of a piece — all of a Place. And it always had been and always would be, for what would change it? Stability, familiarity, sustainability — we are born expecting these aspects of our homes. It's only natural. Or was. But how many today know this incredible immeasurable depth of immersion in one place? Few. And growing fewer. Change of the land and loss of Place is not just the nature of our modern growth-economy culture, it is our culture. Yet stories, meaning, Place — these are the true "traditional uses" of land that precede all others. And supercede all others, in the radical politics of my mind.

Afternoon: Mark and I hike high into the bowels of a deep canyon. Even in the farthest recesses we find evidence of what in the politics of public-lands policy are called "traditional uses": cowpies lining pounded cowpaths. Mark curses as he kicks the sloppy paddies aside for a place to have lunch. I'll be honest, though: Given a choice, I'll take cowflops over mountain bikes. Or at least over the industrial recreation industry and its crowds, fees, reservations, management, marketing, improvements, policing, and general commercializing of the outdoor experience — the Disney Wilderness. Ideally, of course, like the bumpersticker I plan to market one day will say, "I'd rather be hunting and gathering." But the reality is we live in an age of triage: we gotta pick the lesser of evils, and hold that ground, for the time being.

Here's my triage plan: Keep alive the wildness we can — in land and people. That's my fight. That means that even though it sometimes puts me at odds with my eco-friends, I admire and respect those whose ideas of what we should do with our undeveloped landscapes differ from mine, as long as we share the common ground of finding meaning in Place. Chaos and diversity! I don't ask we have the same meaning of Place, it's people who have some meaning of Place who matter to me. It's the spirit to fight for those meanings that I value in people.

So here's my new bumper sticker: "Save the wild people." I envision next to that slogan the picture of a little kid giving the finger.

Sunday: We climb down 1,100 feet of near-vertical cliff-face to the San Juan River. Down to the opaque green flow, a storied flow for me and my wife and our kids and our friends. We slog through the sand upstream until we find a spot where the sun has come around the canyon wall. I strip down and jump in the river; it might be winter, but it's a required and reverent gesture.

I dry off and dress, and join Mark on the warm sand to eat some breakfast. Then, as we sit and nibble and stare, a bald eagle rises from the canyon wall on the other side of the river. He passes no more than fifty feet above us, then circles overhead. As we eat, he takes 15 minutes to slowly and steadily spiral high enough to pass over the canyon rim and out of sight.

"People would pay thousands of dollars to have this moment," Mark says.

"And they still wouldn't have it, because they paid thousands of dollars for it," I say back.

And that's another story.

Much ado about nothing

I'm in Santa Fe, New Mexico, sitting on a miniature patio — two metal chairs and a cheap plastic table — out the back door of my hotel room. The hotel, another in an endless string of Santa Fean mock-adobe retail-chain businesses, is nestled quaintly between a transmission repair place and a row of dumpsters along a busy four-lane whose name for some reason means Street of the Matches.

It is late in the day, cloudy and cold. Rain threatens like a glare.

No other hotel guests sit on any of the couple-dozen other little back-door patios today. Why would they? It's winter and cold and darkening and there's nothing going on. There's nothing here. There's nothing to do. Of course, the corporate inn-keepers at this road-side lodging establishment anticipated this situation: back through the sliding-glass door in my motel room, as in every room here, is a big TV that receives 68 channels (with the option of paying to view any number of movies), a radio, and complimentary copies of the Albuquerque Journal, Newsweek, and Santa Fe magazine, which lists everything I could be doing in Santa Fe but am not. I'm not because I'm out here, in the cold, where no normal person was, is, or would be.

In fact, that's why I'm out here.

I'm doing nothing myself. My view is an enclosed concrete courtyard populated by a few empty chairs and an unused swimming pool that steams like a fresh carcass. But this is not what I look at. I stare at the sky: it is a mottled swirl of grayscale waves and eddies and streams and hanging streamers backlit by the lowering sun. I can't get enough of this sky and the winter cold descending toward earth like a fallen angel. With my hands in my pockets and my pile jacket zipped to my chin, I savor the chill. I study the wrinkles and rolls of the low clouds like a lovely land-scape. I do this for a long time, and for that whole time not a single other person steps or peers out of the many doors around me.

I am used to this.

For example: It's mid-summer, and I'm in a canoe in the middle of a lake, somewhere in the Northwoods. There's no one else out here — but why would there be? It's midnight. Even though during the day the lake hums like a mall with water skiers and trolling fishermen and party barges, there's not much going on in the middle of this lake in the middle of the woods in the middle of the night. That, of course, is why I'm out here. It's not that I don't want people out here — I think anyone else I'd meet sitting silently in a canoe on a lake at midnight would be someone I'd like to meet — but I tend to find that those things other folks aren't doing are sometimes good things to do. Things most people consider "doing nothing."

Here's the nothing I find this night: A single, lone wolf howl. Occasional startling bursts of loon calls, like oozing hoots. A full moon so gleaming and brilliant it hurts to look at. A lake surface so perfectly flat and glassy that it seems like a betrayal to carve a paddle into it. So I don't. I just sit. Look. Smell. Feel. Try to peer into the eerie shadowline below the moon-lit treetops, a dark hat-band ringing the lakeshore. And I ponder why there's not another person in a canoe — or 800 other people in 800 other canoes — also sitting silently and savoring this glorious gift of nothingness this night on this lake offers.

But I know why. How could I persuade them, even if I wanted to?

"What were you doing out there?"

"Nothing."

"What was out there?"

"Um, nothing."

Even back in my hometown of Durango, a town chock-full of

self-proclaimed get-away-from-it-all-ers and road-less-taken takers, I frequently find myself alone in situations rich with nothingness.

For example: It's another full moon, this one beaming down like a cop's searchlight on the year's first glistening snowscape. It's very cold, and the snow squeaks like styrofoam under my pack boots. I wear thick skiing mittens, a wool cap with the Avalanche logo stitched on the front, and the warmest jacket I could find buried in my backcountry-gear box. Even my beer needs help: my can of Bud wears a coosie to keep from freezing.

Under these most unalluring of conditions, I go for a long walk. I stroll along the rim of the college mesa, while below me, downtown glistens like Atlantis under a shallow pool of wood-stove and train-smoke smog. Behind town, where things are going on, is nothingness: The hogback, striped by snow like a lying tiger; Perins Peak, a great luminescent bridal gown of snowy slopes; and in the distance, the moon-lit La Platas glowing like a rumpled sheet under a black light. It's fantastically, fantasmagorically beautiful. Surreal. Super real. And, as near as I can tell, no else is seeing it.

By why would they? All these ventures into nothing take thoughts normal people don't think: like dressing up like one of Shakleton's shipmates just to walk a trail above town when you could be watching the NFL's special presentation of Thursday night football ... or dragging your lazy ass from the front of the fireplace and declining your lovely wife's invitation to bed so you can paddle out on a lake at midnight ... or sitting solemnly alone in the cold dusk outside of a hotel room like some creepy loner.

These are just not things normal people do. This is just not how we're raised in a culture where "to get out" means to do something, and where "something" is always extreme and usually costs money — that's how you know you're not just doing nothing. And normal people don't do nothing for fun.

Look at the ads: you ride your mountain bike to jump and rip and grind the trails; you drive your truck to rip and grind and bump the tundra; you meet women to bump and grind and rack up the trophy; you build your house and buy your car and dress and go places to make your lifestyle a trophy. "Normal" in our culture means everything must be something — dramatic, cool, in crowds, and to the max — for it to be worthwhile. In our culture, "nothing" is not normal.

Fortunately, I've never been accused of being normal.

This is me: A newly-made acquaintance and I are talking about our boating careers, and, of course, the conversation inevitably shifts to whitewater ... the big holes we've bombed, the involuntary swims we've swum, the gnarly rock gardens we've tackled, the big rocks we've biffed. Seems that when you're talking about boating, that's what you talk about.

So I take the plunge. I admit it: "You, know, I'm really ... just a floater."

This is followed by a pregnant pause in the flow of conversation, like I'd just admitted a sexual preference for barnyard animals.

Onward I plunge. "I really prefer to just sit on my boat, sliding down the river on flatwater, maybe sipping a beer or scribbling in my journal, but mostly just doing ... nothing."

Another pause and stare, like I'd just admitted a preference for my companion's animals.

Then a smile. Then this acquaintance says, "Yeah. Me, too." Then we laugh.

And then we say nothing. Then we just sit there awhile, nothing being said, comfortably saying nothing.

And it's that nothing that makes me think that maybe this new friendship is something.

Dive bombed

*L*et's get right to the point: There's just something about a dingy bar. I'm not sure what it is, really, but I've always been drawn to that natural "rustic" feel of a dive – those worn hard-wood floors, that 45-watt bare-bulb lighting, the bartop as cigarette-burned as a Sandanista rebel, those peanut shells absorbing the spilled Coors under the duct-taped legs of butt-scarred barstools. I can't say I'm really proud of it, but that's my kinda' place, especially when the backcountry is locked in by winter and the wildest country around is behind a neon sign and battered door.

I've had many favorites. And like favorite rivers, much-loved stretches of canyons, worshipped cirque valleys and bald peaks, my most adored dive bars are remembered with treasured tales of wildness, adventure, and honest characters.

My first real love affair was with the Crooked Creek Saloon, in Fraser, Colo. There were lots of other firsts here, too: I first stumbled through its doors on one of its infamous 25-cent draw nights, locally known as "Wednesday Night at the Fights." This led, over several years' worth of Wednesdays (and Thursdays, and Fridays, and ...), to, among other intriguing firsts: the first time meeting my wife, the first time another couple tried to pick up me and my wife, and, later, my wife's getting me drunk enough to agree it was time for us to get pregnant.

The Crooked Creek is also the first (and only, so far) place where I have danced on a table in front of a room full of cowboys and ski bums with a professional belly dancer. I'm not sure why there was a belly dancer in the

Crooked Creek on one of those 25-cent draw nights, but one Wednesday night, there she was, with bells on. Literally. And all kinds of spangly jangles and sheer colorful scarves and some kind of exotic short skirt and not much else.

Or so it seemed after about $2.50 worth of 25-cent beers, when for some cosmic reason I may only discover when I die, she wiggled her nervous navel through the testosterone-reeking crowd (both male and female) right to me. She shook herself down to my sitting level, her bare belly quivering like the inside of my brain, grabbed me by my flannel shirt with one ring-covered bedeviled finger, and lifted me (for even gravity offered no resistance) up to the top of the table, where I (I was told repeatedly for days afterward, so it must be true) danced an exotic and erotic sort of Hillbilly Baghdad Rag.

Of course (and fortunately), there were other denizens of the Creek far more colorful than I. Like JC.

I first met this long, lean high-country wrangler when I stumbled into a keg party at his cabin (I can't quite remember how I ended up there) in the moribund railroad hamlet of Tabernash (home to only a liquor store and tackle shop, but what else did we need then?). Even though JC and I were as unlikely compadres as Larry Flint and Jerry Falwell sharing mint juleps, somehow that night we found an issue that concerned us both: the light pollution from Tabernash's half-dozen or so streetlights blurring our view of the moon-lit Continental Divide. We bonded, Colorado cowboy and Boston ski bum, during the wee-est of the wee hour. As we strolled through our humble little town, while JC carried the keg and I a slingshot, we took turns extinguishing those evil and needless streetlights (there is no traffic in metro Tabernash), toasting a beer after each kill.

JC earned his full membership as a dive character, though, one night while I was driving the local late-night bus. My route took me down a county road, left onto U.S. 40, past the Creek, and back to Winter Park Ski

Area. When I stopped at the county road's stop sign, my headlights beamed directly into the backside of the Crooked Creek.

This particular night it was snowing one of those heavy, dreamy, swirly, nearly opaque snowstorms that March brings to the mountains of Colorado. At 9:55, as I stopped and peered down the snow-driven U.S. 40 for oncoming traffic, I saw...or thought I could see...something through the snow, out behind the Crooked Creek. Something seemed to be lying there in the drifts, like maybe a dog the size of VW van. Then the snow spun in like a white dust devil and it was gone. I made my turn and was gone, too.

10:55. I rumbled down through a deepening snowpack to the terminus of C.R. 8 again. Stop. Look. Then there it was again ... or something was: this time I thought I could see a bunch of people hunched down in the whiteout, leaning together in a tight circle like the ghosts of the 1928 Chicago Bears. Then, again, the snow absorbed the scene like a fading TV station and the apparition was gone.

11:55. The snow had let up considerably, allowing me to see a good 50 yards down the road, although where exactly the road was amidst the great white dunes was hard to say. This time I was already anxious to see what spectres might materialize behind the Creek when I arrived at the end of the county road. And, sure enough, there was something there. But what the hell was it? This time no ghostly football team, no sleeping dog the size of an automobile ... but there was definitely something there ... something reddish and mottled like a Navajo blanket lying in the snow....

My bus was empty, so I decided to check it out. I pulled up across the highway and into the dark lot behind the bar until my high beams finally illuminated the mystery mound: Lying there in the snow was the partially snow-covered and fully skinned carcass of a horse.

I heard the full story the next day. Late that previous night, JC's horse — which, using wise rural logic, he regularly rode the five miles from Tabernash to the Crooked Creek to avoid DUIs — had gotten loose and been hit by the train. A sad affair, for sure, but JC was not a man without feelings: he and his cowpoke buddies skinned the horse so JC could make a jacket to honor his fallen steed. Not a man without compassion, as well, he named his next horse "Car Target." "Reverse psychology," he explained to me, nodding his grungy leather sombrero smartly.

Although the Crooked Creek will always hold a special place in my heart and liver, there have been others. During my river-guiding years, there was The Green Parrot, in Buena Vista. Here the river-guiding crew I worked with pooled and then pissed away our tips, whiling away the hours until we were ready to drive up to our impromptu tent village hidden away in the Collegiate Peaks. Another cowboy bar, it took a while for our kind to be welcomed there, but enough pool games and shared pitchers of Coors, and we soon became part of the Parrot scene. Although not as much as "Merle." We never got his full name, because the only thing this campeñero seemed capable of saying was "Meeeeeerrrle Haggard!"

Merle was there every night, all duded up in his pearl-button cowboy shirt with the embroidered picture of Merle Haggard on the back, his big silver rodeo-style Merle Haggard belt buckle, and his Stetson with the leather Merle Haggard hat band. All night every night he dropped quarter after quarter into the jukebox so we could all become enlightened from the insights found in Merle Haggard classics such as "Branded Man," "Shade-tree Fix-it Man," and "Tonight the Bottle Let Me Down."

Merle, of course, wasn't playing a full discography in his own mental jukebox. Try to invest a little variety by putting on some R.E.M. or Bad Company or even Johnny Cash, and Merle would simply unplug the jukebox, plug it back in, then plug in enough quarters for a half-dozen sequential listenings of "Okie from Muskogee." Served us right. But nobody minded; Merle was part of the Parrot, and everyone loved him, let him sit with them, bought him beers, and cheered and toasted to Meeeeeerrrle Haggard! with him. He had a home and family there.

Where else? Juanita's, in Boulder, was our wintering ground for a while, while my wife and I studied at the University of Colorado between river seasons. A more sophisticated establishment than the Creek or the

Parrot — you could tell by the green neon cactus that glowed importantly from one corner of the room — Juanita's was home to several important events in my life: It's where we and our mourning friends went to toast Ed Abbey's death — the first Ed Abbey Party, which we still hold every spring. It's also where I went to celebrate defending my master's thesis (the topic: Why some journalists — I nominated myself — should refuse to be objective). That's also the last time I wore a tie. It disappeared sometime during that all-night celebration, last seen being worn by the neon cactus. I never bothered to replace it.

And today? Where do I go now that I live in Durango when winter's long, dark cold drives me indoors, to the wilderness within?

Where else? Ever since I first rolled into town more than ten years ago, the historic El Rancho Tavern has quenched my affection (affliction?) for good, quality, dive atmosphere and dive-loving companions as classless as myself. It's like coming home: the swirling blue cigarette smog, the dangerously cheap beer specials (no more 25-cent draws, but still bargains), the shameless unselfconscious yelling and laughing and backslapping patrons sipping shots and shooting pool — somewhere in there are Durango's JCs and Merles. It's even got a few nice touches that make it unique: the best damn jukebox in the Four Corners, sharp-tongued no-bullshit waitresses, and bottomless bowls of stale popcorn for absorbing those shots of Hornitos that so effectively improve my pool playing (it's a psychological fact: recall is best achieved in the same state as the learning).

It's not the Creek, but it's home. Like Meeeeerrle Haggard sings:

I've got swinging doors, a jukebox and a barstool
And my new home's got a flashing neon sign
Stop by and see me anytime you want to
'cause I'm always here at home 'til closing time

Seeing the light after the fire

I can't pretend to know what it was like to have watched fire approach. But I can imagine: First, a smoke plume signals from over the hill. Then an opaque wall of cloud pulses and pumps from behind the ridge. This is inevitably followed, despite the shields of hope you and your neighbors hold up, by an army of 300-foot pillars of flame cresting the last barrier hill, methodically vaporizing living trees in its path, rolling toward your house, your neighborhood, maybe your livelihood.

I can't pretend to know the feelings of those neighbors of mine who watched the Missionary Ridge Fire move off Missionary Ridge and down into the valleys they call home, eventually devouring more than 70,000 acres of forest, meadow, river drainage, and neighborhood. I, as many of us bystanders did this summer, followed fire's march from a reassuring distance — on TV, on the radio, in the Durango Herald every morning. And from the safety of the Animas Valley, ringed by a rising rampart of grey-black smoke from the cremation of the nearby forests.

I had a good view as the Missionary Ridge fire grew. I work up at the college, on the mesa a few hundred feet above Durango. I saw fire arrive, sort of: first just a single, odd plume of thick smoke atop Missionary Ridge, then within two hours it could've been Mt. Saint Helens brewing up a serving of lava. The next day, it menacingly wore its own personal war bonnet of a cumulus cloud, as the line of smoke crawled up the

Florida Valley.

As the fire spread, I tried to envision its awe-instilling and gut-ripping power. I tried to comprehend what could suck in the atmosphere and spit out tornadoes. I tried to picture the scene as it confiscated the sun and replaced it with its own corona of light and heat. I tried to psychoanalyze it as it was born, grew, evolved, threw tantrums then rested, and then was kicked back into its erratic, unpredictable moods by the slightest nudging of the wind.

I could picture those things — tangible, physical experiences. But the feelings of the people in the path lay beyond the scope of my empathy.

I can't pretend to have heard the sirens signaling that it's finally time to get the hell out of there, now, with whatever or nothing, just get outside and into the car and go, immediately, without looking back. Or, if you stayed to fight, as some did, I can't pretend to know what it was like to see firefighters arrive in their barnstorming battalion of ragtag fire-fighting vehicles — like those Massachusetts farmers jogging up to face the bristling, formal, intimidating lines of British Redcoats on the bridge over the Concord River.

For many it was a war, hand-to-hand combat. From town, though, it was more like Bosnia in the 1990s, as slurry bombers flew those low-level north-south patterns for raids out in the country. I stood on my porch and tried to imagine what it was like to watch thankfully as those bombers dropped their fat, fluorescent slurry strips across people's back yards. But I couldn't imagine the gut-filleting feeling as fire leapt and stepped and crawled across those barriers as if they were speed bumps.

I can't pretend to know what it was like to have fire come to stay, because my family and I were never evacuated, pre-evacuated, or potentially evacuated. The closest fire actually got to our house in town was a light and brief flurry of ash when it crested Missionary Ridge, several miles away.

But I do know what it's like to have fire drop by for a visit.

Ours was an unexpected house call — no watching fire fan out after emerging from some sipapu-like spark. No following updates on *durangoherald.com*. No firefighters hacking a defensible perimeter around the house. The firefighters came, but only in time for the show, and got no further than wetting down the embers. Although: to add onto the well-justified piles of praise heaped on the Missionary Ridge firefighters, the local volunteers who came to our fire incredibly went into our burning house to pull out our photographs and CDs. They could see them through our front windows. They knew we'd want them, one of them explained simply, when my wife and I went up and stammered, Why? We then stammered, Thank you. Thank you.

Fire, though, had vanished by the time we arrived. No wondering, worrying, fretting about what if? We just came home and fire had come and gone, leaving us its signature ash and calling-card charcoal, and not much else — a blackened frame of wood sizzling in a deep bowl of February snow, like a ridiculous version of one of those big bonfires we used to build on the snow while ice fishing. We returned from a lovely afternoon snowshoe in the woods to find our material world reduced to the level of the Bronze Age.

A disturbing thing. But this was particularly problematic because not only did we still have to go to work eventually, even though all we now owned only was what we had worn that day (and why, exactly, did I choose to wear suspenders?). Our situation, particularly the homeless part, was further complicated by my wife's being six months pregnant.

Interlude: Let me note here that this is the first time I have ever written about this event. Frankly, it was just too intense to want to relive — and living life again is one of the reasons I write. But this was just too bitter to bother. A poet friend of mine caught it well, though. Gregory Moore came by the fire the next day and walked slowly through the wreckage while Sarah and I were out somewhere (we wanted to be anywhere but there). He then when home and wrung his experience out of his skin and onto the page. Nothing like poetry to capture sensations beyond the brain's ability to process.

Here's what he wrote:

aftermath

I come just to see, and am conquered
by a simple stream of dripping water...
a persistent sound, amidst the quiet
of a house abandoned;
a light drumbeat in the silence
of a light and snowy morning,
coming from a rend in the roof
where the rafters burned away.

A pair of shoes, a purse,
a shelf of blackened books
I recognize as yours ...
the possession of all the rest,
twisted and singed, indeed gone
for the most part or dropped
to the blackened soil where the floor
vanished in the heat,
undebatable, given the fate
in all its quick striking madness.

Mute, in witness to what must have been
the rushing road of an afterburner,
I walk the perimeter yellow-ribboned by firemen,
head filling with that odor you will never forget,
wondering what in the world I will say when I see you ...

wondering why the firewood stack
in its curl of cast iron
remains untouched, so just-split clean,

wondering where your new baby will sleep,

and wondering, walking like a drunk
through tears and broken glass,
how I can feel like all is lost
knowing all of you, and all our love
are together and well, still alive.

No, I can't know what it was like to have been hit by the Missionary Ridge or Valley or Million or any of the too-many other fires that have visited us this summer. But I know what it's like to have your home taken away as well as anyone. Too well.

So, back to our story: What else could we do? We placed our remaining earthly possessions into the back of our Subaru (it all fit, with room for the dog) and went out into the world. And this was the biggest lesson: We may have been suddenly, unexpectedly impoverished, but we were not poor, as we would soon learn in abundance.

That night, we had dinner and a bed, care of our neighbors who acted like it was obvious that we'd have dinner and a bed in their home. Thank you, Steve and Stacie.

Within 24 hours, we had a room to live, free of charge, with another pair of friends who made it seem like the room had been reserved in advance. Bless you, Wendy and Mike.

In the next few days, clothes appeared on our new doorstep and materialized at work and arrived in big boxes from old friends and relatives and friends of relatives. We will never forget you, whoever you are.

For the next month acquaintances we'd been too busy to maintain contact with asked us out to dinners like we did it every week and it was their turn to buy. Friends then, and now.

Within two months, a woman who raised her family in town in a old Victorian house sold it to us, turning down offers from realtors and out-of-towners $20,000 and $30,000 more than we could muster, because, she said, "This house deserves a family." You are a goddess, Shannon.

In three months, we were back in the 20th century. And our soon-to-arrive family had a home again to arrive to.

So maybe I know something that many of those people who lost their homes to this summer's big fires are now learning: As George Carlin once joked, but sagely, a house is just a place to keep your stuff. And inside it is just ... stuff. Cliché, but true: as long as you, or anyone else you love, had the good fortune to not be inside that house when fire came by, it's just stuff.

In three months, we had lost our home but discovered our tribe. Our community. We were reminded that we belonged to a community. We learned that some friends are obvious — there every day, and there when you need 'em, in spades; but some friends are like spadefoot toads — living underground, but still alive, just waiting for a storm to beckon them emerge.

These were the unexpected lessons fire taught us that we have never forgotten.

When our world burned, we learned our world was a lot bigger, a lot deeper, a lot more solid than we'd realized. We've never forgotten the impaled-feeling of our house fire, but we also haven't forgotten the healing of the aftermath. And I've seen that, too, in the wake of this summer's fires. And on a scale much, much grander than we experienced.

So this summer, my sincere admiration goes out to the firefighters, and the many other individuals and agencies, who rose to anchor those with lives uprooted by this summer's fires. My sympathy — and, as much as possible, my empathy — goes out to those people who lost their homes.

And to people, like us, fortunate enough to not know what it was like to have fire visit this summer, I'd like to point out that this, still, is all our chance to appreciate the difference between what's just stuff, and the stuff fire can't touch.

Home is where the tent is

*I*t was May when I had my mid-life crisis. I was lucky: It happened on a weekend, and my friend Spinner had his at the same time, so we got to do it together. And our wives were away on a river trip without us, so they were lucky, too. Or strategic.

On that fateful weekend, Spinner and I found ourselves home alone for three days and three nights with our kids, a challenge that was compounded by the discovery that because of this sudden ambushing by our mid-life crises, we craved to be somewhere, anywhere, as long as it was Down the River. Any river. We also found this urge to be so very compelling that if we were inside the house for more than minutes at a whack, we were, like old salts everywhere, overcome by the overwhelming need to do a shot to knock down the psychically gnawing call of the water.

So that's how it became imperative for us to stay out-of-doors, so as to avoid some rather depressing and drunken mid-life doldrums, which also would've not been very conducive to good parenting, with still three days to go and all.

Spinner's mid-life quandary manifested thus: Why must I be Here rather than *out there* all the time?

My question bore a slight spin, but targeted the same heart: Why can't here just feel more like out there all the time?

Once again, we were lucky. More out of necessity than any kind of mystical insight, and without really trying, we found that the solution to our indoor problem also answered both our questions.

Since we couldn't go inside without the risk of becoming sociopaths, we set up our tents in Spinner's down-town backyard (just four doors down from ours) and for three days, right in our own neighborhood, we stalked what Spinner, in his distinctly carpenter's Zen way, calls "the grain of the world." I'm still not sure what it means, but it sounds profound enough to be true.

Whatever it is, the kids loved it. It's amazing no one called Social Services: With Maddie looking like some midget hippie-chick in her tie-dyed long t-shirt dress with red-yard belt, yarn bracelets and anklets; with the all-boy Webb in a Bulls' uniform and a too-big Denver Nuggets cap; with Jack sporting a Barney costume; and Anna a little mountain girl under a Huck Finn straw hat — and the whole lot of us barefoot — we must've looked like the Lost Tribe of Berkeley circa 1969.

Even though we were in town, we were on a backcountry mission: For three days we headed off on around-the-block ventures, piecing together mental maps of the town as a landscape rather than a cityscape. We hiked the alleyways, trails, sidewalks, and lawns. We entered stands of trees and traced drainage ditches through the neighborhoods. Sometimes Spinner and I would just follow the kids, seeing the cityscape like they do: just more landforms to wander around.

Frequently we would stop to take turns pointing things out to each other: We learned what trees shade the street and what plants inhabit the dark spaces between houses. We figured out what animals frequent the alleys and what birds hang out over Spinner's house. (We found they're mostly ravens, and that they shit all over Spinner's car, no matter what side of the street he parks on. In our enlightened states, we figured this must be some kind of sign, but perhaps we're better off not knowing for sure.)

We quickly relaxed into this "camping under the mesa," as we started calling it, and ended up having a truly splendid, wild, adventurous three days. I still have a short, cryptic note I scribbled in a pocket notebook sometime that weekend. It says:

At home. Have tanned feet and sunburned brain.
Children growing increasingly feral.

The kids didn't find any of this the least bit odd or disturbing. But why would they? This is what kids do from the moment they reach mobility. I remember one of my first experiences with this, when Webb first entered toddlerdom. It took me a long time to get anywhere those days, but I didn't mind. The pace was worth the anchor I was dragging — an almost-two-year-old boy who couldn't put together a dozen steps without finding something worth a long, slow, detailed inspection.

Every evening before dinner, Webb and I bundled up and wandered out. Our goal was humble: to circumambulate at least two of our little city's blocks. This world is your basic cityscape of sidewalks, houses and hedges, cats and dogs and crows and parked cars, but with my little partner's illuminating, it transformed for me on those afternoon saunters. Webb didn't do anything magic to cast this spell; he just acted his age.

One night he came to me clasping a captured pine cone. He had no word for pine cone, so he used the Toddler's Generic Word, "dah....," but with an inflection that said, "Dude! Check this out!" He wanted me to share in his discovery, so with a smile like it was his birthday he held the pine cone aloft while I bent down to study it. I looked it over. I touched and turned it. I held it up to the light. But I saw only a pine cone, like every other pine cone. I handed it back to him. He insisted I pocket it, looking a little exasperated, like he thought maybe if I mulled it over awhile I'd see what he saw later.

That was pretty much the norm on our ventures. We walked and stopped and this little three-foot man would reverently hand me an endless stream of sticks and litter and stones. I quickly became his porter.

It wasn't just graspable things that captured Webb's attention. Birds were important; I hadn't noticed until then how many ravens share our neighborhood. Trees were always worthy of a passing touch or pat; it seems tree-hugging is in our genes. The boy also had an early affection for machinery. He had an acute ability to pick out planes, and practically danced a jig every time he saw a bus or a tractor-trailer. I must admit it: his enthusiasm was contagious. More than once in that first year of toddler-fatherhood, I caught myself excitedly pointing out a school bus to a concerned friend.

Even though I couldn't always muster the energy to share his awe over every broken branch or chunk of cement, he managed to recast for me what was just "the neighborhood" into a complex and complicated world full of little events and fine details. And this, I believe, was a good thing. Why? While it's tempting to get all romantic and philosophical, I think the lesson here is simple. I think this little two-block world was so special to Webb not because he saw things I, as an adult, couldn't, but because he didn't yet have an adult-style value system telling him what is and isn't worth seeing. As a two-year-old, Webb held no definitions yet of what comprises a pretty rock, or rare bird, or funny car (although he did laugh and point at Volkswagen Beetles). To him, everything was worthy of notice and appreciation.

It's a lesson worth learning. And it affected me: Even though I'm a pretty busy guy, I still find myself nodding to the ravens, acknowledging the variety of trees on our street, and sauntering along the alleys rather than buzzing down the quickest route to town. And years later, this view made having my mid-life crisis while home for three days with four kids in my friend's backyard become something I want all the time anyway: another intriguing and adventurous foray in the great safari of life.

On the last night of our neighborhood adventure (although I'm not that sure it has really ended), while our exhausted, happy, dirty kids snored away in their tents and Spinner and I toasted a beer around a campfire in the Weber grill, my friend offered up his trademark single-sentence summary of our long weekend: "I now realize that the grain of the world is in Durango, too."

What's the grain of the world? I still had no idea. But no matter — I was with him.

"I know," I said, as we toasted our beers. "And there's grain in beer, too. That's why it's good."

We toasted again.

"They don't sell this feeling at Wal-Mart," he continued.

"If they did, there'd be a governmental warning," I answered. "Caution: these sensibilities have been known to cause pantheism, anarchy, tribalism, insubordination, indolence, and daily napping in otherwise productive citizens."

"Well, there must be a city ordinance or a federal law or something against this."

"If there is, then they're gonna start calling your house 'The Compound' in the Herald."

Then we were quiet for a while, and it felt surprisingly like we were camped on the river. We watched the almost-full moon glisten through the juniper next to Spinner's house. We sipped our beers and listened to the Grateful Dead Hour on a little radio as Jerry urged us to wake up to find out we are the eyes of the world. Streetlights glared, cars grumbled, dogs barked, doors slammed — for a while, though, all these urban intrusions seemed more like mere circumstance, an element of what is. It all seemed like out there.

"If this is my mid-life crisis," Spinner finally said, smiling into the city night, "make mine a double."

Back to the hunt

I sit on a rocky hillside, a seat scraped out of the dirt behind and under a big spade-shaped juniper. This is piñon-juniper country, but sparse and open from a beetle-kill, the victims standing across the hillside as heaps of weathered bones clawing the air. This openness allows me several straight shots down the slope and across the cut of an old irrigation ditch that runs the length of the valley, and also along which runs a game trail speckled with a strings of deer tracks like the imprints of fallen leaves.

This valley doesn't earn many points on the grandeur scale - just a long and shallow draw harboring a perennial ribbon of water (sacred stuff in this semi-arid land) and scattered clusters of scrub oaks and cottonwoods. Nothing anyone will throw a national park up around anytime soon. But in the past few days I've walked this draw a half dozen times, wandering slowly, deliberately, along different routes each time, studying everything, drawing up detailed and connected mental maps. I've come to know it intimately, to even understand it some, I think. When hunting, this is what you do. Especially bow hunting, where you have to get close for a shot at an animal.

Bow hunting also means I sit a lot, hopefully letting the animals come to me. And I've done that, too, especially at dawn and dusk, like now. Just sitting, watching, waiting for ... anything. I try hard to carry few preconceived ideas about what might happen out here, because it's near-impossible to predict from where a deer might step, or how it might look when it appears, or how skittish it'll be as it moves. When hunting, to expect something is to miss something. I need to just focus and observe, make my eyes and ears and nose and even my skin one big radar dish, scanning, scanning....

I mostly stay focused on this task. Still, no matter how much I want to hold my gaze down those shooting lines, my eyes keep getting seduced upward, to the treeline across the draw, and outward toward the west and into the staring bloodshot eye of the dry-land sunset. As I sit motionless, the sun rolls off behind the ridge like a nuclear 3 billiard ball, and in its wake cool, sweet puffs of air slide down the valley from the distant Sierra La Plata. Trees stir in the deepening shadow-cast. A few blocky bergs of clouds, their weighty bottoms torched as they drift eastward, melt in an ice-blue twilight sky.

I sit on.

I sit on until birdsong evolves into frog chorus. Until the rose dome of sunglow deflates into star-punctured twilight. Until a deer would have to be glowing for me to actually take a shot at it (and after reading Carlos Castaneda, I'd have a hard time shooting a glowing deer). Until there's nothing left to do but go.

Well, no deer tonight, I think to myself walking back to camp through the dim dark. Still, though, I feel like I bagged something out here.... a feeling of being alive ... a sense of this unappreciated place where I have come to know most every topographic wrinkle and biotic blotch ... a taste of a day ... a single solar pass in which I was fully *there*....

Some fine, worthy scores, I think, although they may be a tough sell with my wife, greeting me at the door with empty skillet in hand. But at the risk of rhapsodizing philosophic, let me posit that the finest rewards of the hunt come from the *hunting* — that living only in the moment through sharp, observant, and open-minded poise, patience, perseverance, and presence — the traits it takes to be successful when doing the death-dance with smart, elusive animals. Necessary traits in the field. Worthwhile character traits for a lucid life anywhere, even life in a culture in which we don't *have* to hunt.

Perhaps these are character traits our consciences are genetically programmed to aspire to, following that remnant programming from a time when we couldn't afford to stroll back from the hunt to family and tribe empty-handed but waxing philosophic, like I do now, thinking hard and threading my way cautiously through this ghost land to my camp and a beer, hamburger, and comfortable campfire. For our hunting and gathering ancestors, a strong character was pragmatic, both requirement and reward for survival skills.

My own high-falutin' rhetoric aside, I must admit that I, too, came out here for more pragmatic reasons than to aspire to some sort of paleolithic sainthood. All those deep thoughts came later, discoveries made while I was already out stumbling around, meeting other agendas (as most big discoveries come). What really got me here was a simple question from my four-year-old boy.

"Dad, who killed this chicken?" Webb asked me one otherwise innocuous night, holding up his barbecued drumstick to make sure I knew what triggered his query.

Now, I realize I tend to think too much (as my wife always tell me), but this simple question paralyzed me. His first questions, when he was two and three years old, had been so cute and easy to field. "How come we don't have tails?" he asked me at two, and at three, "Why do we have two eyes?" He even asked me at three and a half, "Where does milk come from?" I thought I handled that one pretty well, even without the visual aids it would've been nice to offer with the explanation. But for the chicken question I couldn't devise a quick answer that I could sneak past the customs of my conscience. What do I say? A *farmer*? For gods' sakes, I reprimanded myself, the slaughterhouse laborer who ended this chicken's life and began its long mechanized journey to our kitchen is about as much a "farmer" as the foreman in a toothpick factory is a "woodsmith."

I, of course, still ended up just sputtering "a farmer," then quickly changed the topic so he wouldn't ask me next how this industrial agricultural product probably spent its drugged, incarcerated, pathetic little life.

Webb seemed content with this answer, but the unease from my cowardly deflection lingered. I think too much, I know, but the fact is Webb's question made me realize I *want* to think about who kills my chicken and what its life was like (which, of course, is exactly what the propaganda of packaging and advertising is designed to make you *not* think about).

For a few days after Webb's question, I spent a lot of time just sitting on my front porch staring off at the nearby mountains, wondering how I'm going to teach my little boy that food doesn't come mystically — and bloodlessly — from cans and cardboard containers. Still thinking too much ... but as I stumbled for a philosophical path behind the grocery store shelves, I also stumbled onto some old memories.

When I was ten, my father let me take my bow and go out and shoot a squirrel. I'd been nagging him to do that for some time, but still I was dazzled by actually witnessing the power of an action that up to then had been an abstract game. We stood together over the rapidly cooling little body. Then my dad said, "Now that you've killed something, from now on you have to eat whatever you kill."

And even though I was just a kid, I understood: that death is a responsibility, that food is a necessity, and that respect means to be responsible for the death that is necessary for my food.

That autumn, my father finally took me deer hunting with him. I was unarmed, but still he walked me through the woods by day and he sat me in a tree stand at night, all the while instructing me in the fundamentals of deer and the landscape and how you can figure things out from the interaction of the two. When I was 12, I was first able to actually hunt with a bow. At 14, I was given the responsibility of carrying a gun. These events are and remain the wintermarks of my youth, rites of passage that bestowed power, responsibility, the mystery of connectedness with the non-human world, and senses of both accomplishment and membership in some timeless group of skilled practitioners.

I hunted for several more years as a teen, eventually getting skilled enough to get a close shot at a whitetail. But that's as close as I ever got;

for me, that last stage of this ongoing ritual was never consummated. (I never said I was a *good* hunter.) Once I left the house, I left hunting as well. It wasn't like I really made a decision to give up hunting, it just seemed that as life got busier, not-getting-around-to-hunting slowly lapsed into no-longer-hunting.

About a week after Webb's question, I dug out my old bow and quiver-full of arrows. I stopped hunting years ago not so much because I had a reason to, but more because I didn't have a reason not to. Now I've decided I can no longer afford to not hunt if I want to keep the role of death in feeding my life from being hidden behind grocery store labels and elusive explanations. Although it's not essential that I kill all my food in order to discover the senses of mystery and awareness that come from hunting, it is essential for respect that I take responsibility for at least some of this necessity.

And as a father whose job it is to mentor a little boy in the ways of this world — the living one, not the TV one — then I also can no longer afford to not teach my little boy to hunt.

So, hunting those ends, I return, the hunter's prodigal son, to an old trail, to this ancient ritual. What began as a way to enlighten my little boy has enlightened me — about myself. I find what I really desire is to grow into the type of person worthy of the label "hunter."

Hunting a hunter

*I*⁹ve never met a Neanderthal before. But this might be close.

We walk along a shaded ridgeline somewhere in the southern San Juan Mountains of Colorado on a quickly-cooling late-September late afternoon. We walk quietly, slowly, deliberately, this leading companion of mine and I. We wear full camouflage, from ball caps to pant cuffs, although we are neither hunting nor preparing for some anti-government Armageddon.

We are here together ostensibly for an interview — me as a reporter interviewing a prominent local author. But somehow, due in part to the synchronicity of circumstances in my life and in part to the nature of this nature writer in front of me, this has for me transformed into a walk back in time. Back to my childhood ... and further ... back to the Pleistocene.

Walking ahead of me is David Petersen, one of the nation's leading hunting and wildlife writers. Best known, perhaps, as the editor of Edward Abbey's journals, Petersen also has authored six books of natural history, including the excellent *Ghost Grizzlies*, a report on Colorado's remnant grizzly population. He also edited *A Hunter's Heart*, a controversial anthology on the ethics of hunting that earned him national recognition as a "hunting ethicist, " and he has released *Elkheart: A Personal Tribute to Wapiti and Their World*, a collection of his own essays celebrating elk and hunting.

He is, needless to say, an avid, addicted, and ardent hunter. A bow elk hunter, to be exact. Bow season has just ended, and Petersen spent 24 of its 27 days in the field. Now, his freezer is full of meat. He's a little sad he got his elk with still two weeks left in the season because more and more these days, he explains, "What I want most is the hunt." Still, after his kill, he spent much of the season's last two weeks in the field, unarmed, with hunting friends.

Petersen moves smoothly — no wasted movements, no heavy breath. His fifty-plus-year-old sinewy fame has been sculpted to stalk, his thin, long body conditioned and confident, sliding silently through the woods.

I ask him why the hunt itself is so much more important than the success. He stops and is quiet for a few minutes. He looks around, looking distracted, eyes squinted, bearded jaw moving in thought. He lifts his cap and threads his fingers through the thin hair that rings his bald top.

"These days, I don't know what sort of hunter I am. All I know is, my passions for elk and elk hunting burn hotter than ever. Ironically, though, my passion for the hunt accounts for my killing less and less often, because the killing kills the hunt. The September elk archery season is the apogee of my year, every year. It's one of my life's greatest pleasures."

I stare at him. He stares deeper into the woods.

"We're meant to live the wild, free lifestyles of nomadic hunters and gatherers," he says finally, "earning good honest livings by ambushing mammoths and giant wide-horned bison." He sighs like a retired ball-player remembering the game, then puts his hat back on, turns and walks on up the hill.

This, I can tell, will be like no other interview I've done.

Before we headed into the woods, while inspecting Petersen's little shed of an office — "The Outhouse," he calls it — I spied a photocopy of a "Far Side" cartoon tacked over his desk. It's a picture of a Neanderthal driving a pickup truck with a spear in the gun rack. Below it someone had scribbled "Dave Petersen in a nutshell."

Now I get it.

I've been following Petersen's writings for nearly eight years now, since I first stumbled on his informative, bright little book called *Racks: The Natural History of Antlers and the Animals that Wear Them.* I've read everything he's written since. Over the years, that writing has grown more and more intriguing. Since *Racks*, Petersen's writing's have homed in on a compass bearing his writing will follow in the years to come, he says.

That direction may be best described as, backward with an eye toward the present and future. With his last few books — and especially his latest release — Petersen has carved a niche for himself as a sort of Thoreau with a Bow. Or what a Neanderthal with a pen might sound like.

"This is the place," he whispers finally. We drop down off the ridge to where a spruce has keeled over, it roots leaving a gouge in the ground. This we will use as a blind, he announces as he jumps in and sits in the hole. I climb in. From here we can look down slope to a muddy, shallow spring pockmarked with cloved post holes.

For an hour we sit in silence.

Nope. Ain't never had an interview like this before.

But I have experienced times like this before. Many times. And sitting here, just sitting here, my mind can't help but return to some of those times, other times hunting, back in New England among flashing yellow beeches and aspen-ish birch stands, walking with bow in hand behind my father or, more often, like now, just sitting in silence.

My father would transform at those times. On those excursions I saw my father reflective, reverent, and alert like I never saw him anywhere else. I can still see him stooping to touch and interpret tracks in the duff, his eyes always darting and scanning for movement and message. I can still hear his peculiar whispered statements about our responsibility to the animals and our bond with the land and our human predilection for the woods and the hunt. And it's his image I see in Petersen's face right now.

After an hour we've seen no elk, only a musky stand of gold-coin aspen and dark blue spruce pass motionless through twilight and into night. My notebook is empty of good quotes — we've spoken barely at all — but I've learned much about David Petersen. He turns and grins, obviously not distressed by the failure of his beloved wapiti to appear. "Time for a drink," he says.

In the falling dark, we return to Dave's hand-made "little cabin on a big mountain," as he calls his house. In the yard, he builds a great fire in an old sooty stone ring, and we sit in lawn chairs for the traditional interview portion of my visit. Petersen uncorks a bottle of George Dickel and pours himself a tall one in a plastic cup. I settle on a Budweiser. I offer him one of my cheap grocery store struggling-writer cigars, but he counters with couple of fat successful-writer stogies from some nice humidor somewhere.

In the flash of the firelight, aspens writhe like dancing bones. The scene is set. The interview commences.

Petersen's hunting career began long before his writing career. As a boy in Oklahoma ("Where," he says, "teenagers attend their own family picnics looking for a date"), he first hunted with his father and uncles for small game — "rabbits and squirrels and quail" — and the occasional elusive white-tail deer. But early on, he found the siren call of hunting louder in his ear than those of his companions. When the others got distracted, Petersen headed off to hunt alone.

"From the beginning, hunting for me has been a self-powered passion," he says. "I recall wondering, even then, why I felt such an all-consuming need to hunt. Whatever its motivations, though, hunting has proven a blessing in my life."

And it has developed into a niche in his writing life lately, leading this nature writer to a tribe for which he is story-teller, philosopher, teacher, and — increasingly — conscience: hunters with heart.

"True, ethical hunters may differ in geography, culture, and personal experience, but we are kindred spirits," Petersen explains, "united by our shared love for the chase and all it implies, a love that cuts so deep so that it has to be instinctive."

"Instinctive?" I ask, puffing my big cigar and trying to sound skeptical, trying to sound like a real reporter.

He turns and looks at me. Under his mustache his long, thin ivory smile reflects the firelight. Bull's eye, I realize. A heart shot. I lean back with notebook and beer, and savor the success of the journalistic hunt. Petersen unleashes:

"Millions of years of full-time hunting and gathering, along with the small-group nomadic lifestyle that a foraging life demanded, made us what we are today," he lectures me. "To hunt is to be human. It's our genetic dictum, our generic human heritage, its roots as deep as our time on this Earth. We have not had time in just 10,000 years of agriculture and 5,000 years of civilization to evolve one lonely iota of change in our genome."

"For myself," he continues, "wanting to hunt *well* led me to become a dedicated student of wildness — wildness of all kinds, in life as well as in nature. Setting out originally to just kill and eat, before I knew it I'd become an amateur naturalist and flaming nature lover."

He takes a big luminescent drag on his cigar. "And what we love, we tend to defend."

And Petersen is, if nothing else, a defender. Since his earliest straight-forward nature books, he has been striving to forge a bridge across the chasm between environmentalists and hunters. ("What good do hunters' rights do you if you have no place to hunt and nothing to hunt for?" he asks.) In his recent books, though, that defender is more of a warrior.

In his 1996 book, *A Hunter's Heart: Honest Essays on Blood Sport*, Petersen took a controversial step across that bridge by compiling an anthology of writers urging hunters to self-impose ethical standards of fair chase and limits to technology — standards the growing number of ballot initiatives seek to impose by force — and to become a political force in the defense of wilderness.

While the book received praise, its untraditional message also kicked up a fury of controversy, including a mention in a Time magazine article on the rise in anti-hunting initiatives and an uprising at a major outdoor magazine. When Outdoor Life accepted an essay from the book that criticized the ethics of bear baiting and spring bear hunts, the corporate bosses of the magazine killed the story after being barraged by protests from pro-baiting factions, none of whom had even seen the piece. In response, the magazine's two top editors quit, and in a New York Times interview, one called stopping the story "gutless."

Aside from habitat loss, it's that "gutlessness" among the hunting media and hunters themselves, failing to examine their motivations and ethics, that most threatens hunting, Petersen says. This must change, he argues.

"Too many of today's hunters are way too concerned with acquiring and mastering expensive techno-gadgets. They've been brain-washed to think they can't hunt without all the shit that industry and the media say modern hunting needs. All the while they're ignoring the critical aspects of personal skill and self-reliance," Petersen rants.

Hunters' and the media's failure to stand up against the industrialization of hunting is nothing less than "a collective failure of the hunting spirit," he says, and that in turn is leading to dropping respect, often deserved, for hunting in the non-hunting populace. And this matters, he adds, because this lack of respect is starting to show up at the ballot box.

Hunting must clean itself up, or non-hunters will clean it up for them, "and then some," he says.

"Contrary to what the greed-driven outdoor industry and media would have us believe, we don't need more hunters at any cost; we need better hunters at all cost. Is shooting a bear out of a tree, or with its head stuck in a pail of slop, the sort of hunting 'tradition' we want to fight to the possible death of all hunting to try and uphold? The media are encouraging hunters to hunt with butts and wallets, rather than boots and brains."

Hunters can find the courage to face themselves and their critics, Petersen argues, "if they can be made to see what they're missing by rushing around in a blur of gadgetry and ATV fumes toward what they've been misled to believe is success." To locate that path toward an articulate hunting ethic, Petersen says we can, and must, look back to our evolutionary roots as hunters.

Locating and walking point down that path is the goal of Petersen's work these days. Following up the celebration and defense of ethical hunting begun in the *A Hunter's Heart* anthology, his latest book, *Elkheart*, stands as Petersen's love song to elk and elk country.

This is a rare gem of nature writing: a natural history book that is unusually informative, entertaining, and opinionated, thanks to Petersen's weaving of research, personal experience, philosophy, and humor with some downright furious rants against what he considers to be the more offensive and dangerous threats to wildlife and wilderness. But while *Elkheart* is on the surface a wildlife book, the heart of the book is an exploration of the spirit of the hunter. And it is this spirit, for better or worse, that offers the best hope of saving wildlife and the wild habitat they need to survive, Petersen argues.

"No one, biologists notwithstanding," he writes, "knows or cares more about the natural histories and daily dramas of animals in the wild, no one is a more attentive student of animal spoor, no one more deeply and honestly loves wildlife and wild lands and freedom and dignity, than the true, ethical hunter."

Powerful sentiments, sure to kick up more controversy. And more thoughts.

And that's what happens. We are silent again for a while, and again my thoughts ride away on the campfire smoke. Somewhere up on the ridge we walked a few hours earlier a pack of coyotes yip and hoot in a wild chorus. To the people who inhabited this area for tens or hundreds of millennia, the coyote was a fellow hunter, a comrade with whom to share and learn from; in our present agricultural culture, the coyote is a competitor to be killed.

And my thoughts drift back to just a couple of weeks ago, when I bought my son his first bow. I brought him out with me while I practiced with my bow and I taught him to shoot. I gave him the first of many lessons on respect and care around weapons. I told him for the first time about hunting and how I will take him with me in a few years, as my father had done.

And I wonder for how many millions of years fathers have done the same.

"In each of us still pounds a Pleistocene hunter's heart," Dave says from somewhere on the other side of the fire, pulling me back to the present.

Or is it back to the Pleistocene?

Or is there a difference?

Traveling with trophy travelers

I don't mean to be disrespectful, but ... something about the departure triggered my usually suppressed sense of cynicism.

Ahead lay three days on a cruise ship — a true Love Boat, with 1,200 passengers, 15 decks, and some 400 crew — on a float north along the Inside Passage, from Vancouver to Juneau, and then on to Skagway, Alaska. Nothing to gripe about there. Also, this trip was the most generous gift from my wife's parents, who were taking their entire family, including grandkids — 18 of us in all. Impossible to complain.

But there was something about the departure....

It was just like on TV: neck-thick ropes were tossed from the harbor pier to the boat as the engines grumbled in its belly. A dozen or so left-behind lookers-on waved from the two-level dock, while those of us fortunate enough to be on board toasted back from the rail on the Upper Promenade Deck, complete with swimming pool and outdoor bar serving margaritas and Alaska Brewery beer. In the background, a band played elevator versions of well-known classics that I couldn't quite place.

Sea planes landed gracefully, as if on cue, on the open water in front of the ship. Behind us, the city of Vancouver sparkled under a range of still-snowy summer peaks. And I was right up there with hundreds of other passengers, gathered on the bow deck, sipping weak Margaritas, faces turned into the wind, soaking in the sights.

Yet when I think back on that first fine ship-board hour, rather than festiveness, my memory is of a near-death somnolence — that awkward, shell-shocked atmosphere that only wealthy old white people seem to be able to maintain for any length of time. That isn't cynicism, that's fact: while the paying customers were uniformly pale, the wait staff all seemed to be from the same short, brown Southeast Asian stock. All except for our four peppy Nordic spirit leaders, who leapt into action with a performance of planned-humor introductions and tacky team-building games. These prompted a few loose giggles and overly squeaky squeals, but for the most part even the band whipping into a raucous Muzak version of "Roll out the Barrel" couldn't roust this bunch. Roll out the casket, is more like it.

See. I hate that kind of cynicism.

But this cruise ship stuff was a confusing experience. Yes, over the course of our three days at sea, we could see beauty. As we sailed inside the large islands that line the coast, we could gaze out over ragged rocky island coastlines that jumped right into spruce and fir forest, or we could turn and look inland toward snow-splattered alpine peaks. Spectacular. I learned quickly, though, that the boat itself was the spectacle. Beauty all around, yes. Yes! Stunning beauty. But for most on board (I noticed, as my cynicism again rose like the tide), the outdoor beauty was merely backdrop — just so much more TV. (Or actual TV, if you preferred: in our berth, Ch. 32 was the bow-cam channel, with a 24-hour view from the front of the ship.)

Islands? Ocean? Mountains? Scenery got old? How about the Casino? "A Beautiful Mind" in the theatre? The Country Jamboree? Bingo (deck 5)? Then there's always the five bars. And the free, unlimited food available 18 hours a day. This was a floating pre-school for post-middle agers.

As such, the kids loved it, of course. They were like winos on amphetamines, running bow to stern, hogging the elevators and mowing down geriatrics on the stairs. We'd run into them occasionally, ask minimally-parental questions about whether or not they were tired, if they were causing any problems, how many trips to the ice cream bar they'd made (free, open 18 hours, deck 9). As they stumbled away they would mumble vaguely something about "movie" or "swimming pool" or "game room" (deck 6). It was kid nirvana: a cashless society full of every conceivable urban amenity set in a giant solid enclosure.

As usual, the kids know. Since I was there on that trip to travel, I decided I, too, would put my cynicism aside and revel in the excess: I sampled the abundant food offerings, sipped the many cocktail concoctions, wandered the 15-level wilderness, and mingled with the inhabitants of that strange little floating culture. I went native.

And it was fun and educational. I toasted champagne, along with 300 other passengers, with the Master of our Vessel (as the ship's Captain was introduced) in my $8 Methodist Thrift Store sport coat and new running shoes. My wife and I sipped gin and tonics as we watched the sun set in a chain reaction of wavy sunlight flashes and ripply water-borne sunbeams through the big tinted windows of the Crow's Nest Bar (deck 12). To balance that, we used the health club (deck 10), which was the size of a meat locker stuffed with some weird European kind of workout gear.

"Hey," Sarah came up to me while I tried to do sit-ups without running into another guy's dumb bells. "Have you noticed that the scale registers seven pounds under?"

It all made sense when we learned that the most popular activity offered on board was also in the health club: a clinic called (I swear this is true) "Eat More to Weigh Less."

My brother-in-law and I also got to spend a few hours talking to a few of those Southeast Asian ship staffers. Paul and I were the only attendees at "Cigars Under the Stars" (11 p.m., deck 8), and I'm happy to say that the three crew members we chatted with for a few hours — Ria, Carlos, and Edwin, the bartender, in his eighth year working on ships, just traveling until he takes over his parents' farm — were loving their adventures, like floating Philippino ski bums.

They knew the situation on the boat, but they had a sense of humor about it. As we approached Alaskan waters, my sister-in-law asked one of the crew, "Where's the best place to see whales?"

"On the Lido Deck," he replied.

This seemed odd to her, since the Lido Deck was enclosed. "Really?"

she asked. "When?"

He grinned. "They eat at the 11 p.m. pizza bar."

I understood the cynical humor reflected here. Most of the people on this cruise were here for the excursion into excess more than actually getting somewhere and seeing some place. They'd made the money needed to travel like this, and they wanted to spend it. They traveled like they lived: structured, organized, secure, and luxurious. In that type of traveling, it wasn't where you went as much as how you went that mattered. I realized then, though, that I am more akin to the Philippino cruise-ship bums than the people they waited upon.

Pretty fun and insightful stuff. And this "traveling" attitude got me along for a few days. By day three, though, I was rabid as Cujo. I could not read, sit, walk around, drink, eat, or look longingly at the passing coastline any longer without leaping from the Observation Deck (deck 15). "We could be doing this in Iowa," Sarah muttered as we had another gin and tonic in front of another TV-like window-filtered view of great shadowed peaks. It was time to get off the boat, and out there.

Fortunately, the next morning we arrived in our first port of call. A little water-side city set in a steep fjord, Juneau is surrounded by peaks every bit as radical as the San Juans, reminding me more of Silverton, Colorado, than any other state capital I've ever been to. And like Silverton, I soon realized, we were Juneau's version of money-bearing narrow-gauge train tourists. And I felt like a tourist. But I was happy to get on shore again.

Once Sarah and I got down the gangway, we wandered off into our first Alaskan community. And it was ... like walking around Silverton when the train rolls in: T-shirt shops by the dozen, expensive little American cuisine restaurants, and enough knickknack shacks to keep the Chinese economy afloat.

What did I expect, eh? For all my cynicism, I was one of them: the New Yorkers in New Hampshire, the Chicagoans in Wisconsin, the Texans back home in Colorado. Spend a few hours, get back into your car/RV/train/cruise ship, and head on down the road to your next stop in the itinerary — with your t-shirts and coffee cups and "Alaska" snow-shakers that prove you were there. Trophy traveling.

We buy our trophies — a couple of hats that prove we were there — and mosey bored back to the boat. Like any good trophy tourists, we had a tight itinerary. It was time for our pre-selected "shore excursion": sea kayaking. Now we're getting somewhere! Sea water, close enough to drag my hand in! Actual physical exertion to get somewhere! Out in our own craft! And the place: we paddled across a wide bay to a forested island inhabited by bald eagles and harbor seals. We were there, not just staring longingly from the rail of the ship.

As much as the paddling, though, a highlight was the river people. Like the stubble-faced, joking, local-question-answering bus driver who double-clutched the repainted 1978 BlueBird school bus down to the put in. And our guide, Makaela, sharing with us her stories of the life of the bum traveler — seeing the world by living and working somewhere for a while. This summer it's Alaska; last summer it was guiding river trips in Maine. This winter she was thinking New Zealand. Maybe Costa Rica. After that? She wasn't sure. But she wasn't worried.

My wife and I were river guides for several years, living out of tents and mountain shacks for those summers. And this only reminded me that river guides, like ski bums, like any kind of bum travelers, are the same everywhere: they go somewhere to be somewhere, to actually be in a place rather than at a place, to experience for a while the life that makes a place a place. Like our new-found Philippino friends back on the boat. Like Makaela.

Like the helicopter bum we met in Skagway the next day. Our shore excursion here was "the glacier sightseeing helicopter flight." Truly amazing. Beyond description. At one point, Eric, our pilot, landed the helicopter on a point of ledge five hundred feet above the junction of two blue-glass glaciers, surrounded by stone-fang peaks rising out of a Pleistocene ice field.

Eric, I learned, got this job after spending a year herding cattle by helicopter on a huge ranch in Texas. "Just flying around," he described it.

This winter he was headed to California to fly down there. Next summer? He didn't know. He wasn't worried.

"Check out that hanging glacier," Eric pointed out across the void of the valley below.

I gave it my Chevy Chase in "Vacation" glance, then turned back to him. "Pretty good job you got, eh?"

"Yeah," he laughed. "Real good."

The bum.

The bum traveler.

That afternoon we left our ship. I was ready. We had another week ahead of us on our packaged tour to head up north, into Canada and northern Alaska. We climbed on the narrow gauge train (see, Alaska is a big Silverton) and chugged up toward White Pass.

I stood outside on the deck between railcars as we rolled out of the backside of Skagway (like how I see so many people leaving Durango every day), out of the tourist-luring zone of wooden recreations of Gold Rush-era-style gift shops and into the unseen side of town. We passed an abandoned railyard, a miners' cemetery, a railroad tie graveyard ... and then we came to still-living tent village — dome tents, canvas tents, makeshift lean-tos, converted-school-bus cabins. Laundry hung on climbing ropes strung between trees. Kayaks lay against trees. A river company's van pulled out of the dirt road.

Bum traveler habitat.

My habitat, I thought, staring longingly as our train chugged onward toward the next stop on our itinerary.

On the river, the kids are alright

*I*t is our third day on the river when we enter the Goosenecks, a 30-or-so-mile section of the San Juan River in southeastern Utah, where for the last several million years the river has tinkered with the project of carving near-perfect backward-and-forward S-shaped meanders in the region's sandstone bedrock.

Pretty special stuff, really. So this morning my wife, Sarah, and I have taken on the project of conveying the marvel of this landscape to Webb and Anna. The hard part is *how*. Our kids are ages six and four, and at that age the earth sciences are a bit abstract for a child's concrete consciousness. Rather than elaborate explanations of their world, kids function under an immediate-presence perception, explaining their world in terms of simple, practical, readily-verifiable actions, reactions, and functions. In a nutshell: children understand their world in operational definitions — function is meaning; function is beauty. And that is good enough.

For example: while Sarah and I babble on about hydrology, Webb and Anna lean over the side out our raft, dragging their little brown hands in the brown river. To them, the "Goosenecks of the San Juan" mean just a gentle back and forth swinging of the river, sunshine, canyon walls of disorderly rock steps, from the rusty-red walls of river level to the distance-blue rim of the distant Cedar Mesa; it means: Sit. Float. Take a turn at the oars on mom's or dad's lap.

We soon get the idea and give up on our explanation project before I can even get to the cool part about "sinusoidal waves." We return to our more pressing daily river chores: Sarah lifts a book and I lift the oars and give a couple of easy pushes to edge ourselves back into the swiftest part of the current. Then I pull the oars back in and look around. And that about fulfills our obligations for the day. That also about sums up our upcoming several days here in the Goosenecks of the San Juan River.

Sound boring? I suppose it is. After a few days on the river, though, you tend to forget that prime directive issued from our media-saturated culture: *Thou shalt not be bored.* On the river, no one, not even the kids, seems to mind this boredom.

The kids tend to keep a bit busier than Sarah and I, actually. This morning, for example, they sing for a while, then act out dramas with Webb's action figures and Anna's dolls, a storyline generally revolving around Spiderman either keeping the Princess Barbie from taking the big swim off the bow of the boat or protecting her from an evil purple lizard man with a long, retractable tongue. This keeps Webb and Anna busy for a while, but, still, as the morning, the hours, the days slide on, they spend a surprising amount of time doing just what Sarah and I do a lot: gazing at the broken-rock talus, admiring the white-sand-over-red-clay beaches, wondering over the swirling and swishing of the river.

"It's like chocolate milk," Webb says at one point, breaking a long silence. I agree. He thinks for a moment. "And the Dolores River looks like Gatorade." Well, yes, I suppose that's true, I answer thoughtfully. And what are my thoughts? I want to further explain to him, and will have to someday, that to some people rivers look like money.

Believe it or not, on the dozens of long river trips we've done with them, the kids have never complained about these empty daily river schedules; we hear more whining about boredom driving to the grocery store twice a week. And this, as anyone who's ever seen Saturday morning TV commercials knows, goes firm-against common wisdom, which dictates that kids today require and demand steady and intense stimulation or else they'll melt down into loud, fleshy versions of the China Syndrome.

Boredom is the reality here, though. In fact, when you do a week on a flatwater river, it's the point. A major — *the* major — part of a long float like this one is just sitting and thinking, looking out over the canyon, looking *into* the canyon. Closely. Repeatedly. On the river, you either learn to stop thinking about what's not here — radio, TV, C.D.s, videos, newspapers, telephones, cell phones, electronic mail, electronic games, electronic shopping, and, of course, the Internet (electronic masturbation) — or you shrivel, quivering and drooling, into the media DTs. As a long-time commercial river guide, I've seen it happen, and it ain't pretty.

The hard thing to remember when you're at home, submerged in all that stimuli, is that the media are not *the* message, as Marshall McLuhan preached; the media simply are *a* message. Just one. Not the only one, and usually not the best one, just a really loud, ubiquitous one. One message from one culture spouting one idea of how to live. And it's everywhere.

Everywhere back there, anyway. Which is why we so often flee for the river. Out here, the only way to avoid the media DTs is to see boredom as an opportunity rather than an ailment. Being bored, really, when you stop avoiding it at all costs, is merely the freedom to surrender your attention to the unplanned, the uncontrolled, the uncontrollable, the unexpected, the unpredictable. What we usually write off as the unimportant: the events of the non-human world. Do that, and you find yourself just ... well, just smelling, listening, feeling. Just breathing. Look at the same old canyon walls or sky or silty river water long enough, and you begin seeking the deeper views, the subtler scents, the slighter sounds and the tenderer sensations — all that background information usually overwhelmed in the static of a "normal" day's business and busyness. These are the news reports our hunter-and-gatherer-evolved senses are designed to read, the Pleistocene mass media.

Now, of course, despite all this enlightened-sounding rhetoric, we really don't just sit here and stare all the time, glassy eyed and with slight all-knowing smiles on our Buddha-like faces. Boredom still eventually drives us to do things. But out here, without all those electronic playthings vying for our attention, we end up doing things we wouldn't do in our normal, civilized world back home. We do spontaneous things ... culturally inappropriate things. We do things like we end up doing now: yanking our boat to shore at the mouth of a recently flash-flooded side canyon, a big fan of rubble and mucky outwash sweeping into the river, and then, all together, kids and all, taking off all our clothes (which ain't much to begin with) and rolling around squealing and giggling in a quarter-acre of soft, deep, oozy, wet mud.

We grown-ups soon have enough mud-play, so we get dressed and set up lunch on the beach while the kids keep on flopping around in the quagmire like eels in a skillet. As all this is going on, from up-canyon suddenly appears a commercial raft motoring by. Yes, motoring, as in a 9.5 h.p. Evinrude. It slows for a moment, then buzzes for the wavy rapid just below where we're stopped. In the back of the boat stands a pudgy, pasty-white guy with a video camera, diligently capturing everything he's missing. No worries; he'll watch it all on TV when he gets home. The three other folks in the boat ignore the rapid and stare at us. Or at the two little naked dirt-brown clay-shaped humanoids dancing around like God's rough drafts of creation.

As I stand and wave at those nice, normal folks getting in their quick blast of river time ("Gotta' get on to Zion tomorrow, honey!") I can't help but wonder what sort of psychological analysis they're drawing up on our feral little family here. But as I look again at our belly-laughing and mud-caked Webb and Anna, I'm not worried. I couldn't explain it in scientific terms, maybe, but I don't need to. As near as I can nail it, this is *my* operational definition of family values.

Just say no, No, NO!

The world,
we are told,
was made for man,
a presumption
totally unsupported
by the facts.

— John Muir

Just say no, No, NO!

*I*t was a sweet summer day, and I was having a lovely walk with a friend down the bike path that runs along the Animas River in downtown Durango.

We soon reached Smelter Rapid, the site of one of Durango's bigger yearly events, Animas River Days, and a stop on the national kayak competition circuit. There we watched kayakers play and surf in the waves for a while, "yeehaw"ed to rafters when a few commercial boats got their customers wet in Smelter's hole, then we moseyed on to nearby Santa Rita Park.

Santa Rita is a nice park, with soccer fields, picnic areas, and a big playground. It's so nice, in fact, that it has become Durango's welcome station of sorts, where tourists first swinging into town can stop and preview some of the town's finer features — views of the nearby mountains, good fishing (this stretch of the Animas is rated Gold Medal Trout Waters), whitewater boating, and kids and adults playing and running around outdoors. It's a compelling ad. Compelling enough, in fact, that the local chamber of commerce built a visitor center here to showcase the Durango lifestyle for prospective tourists. And on this summer day, it was all busy with tourists and locals alike.

These were the pleasant thoughts I was thinking as we casually strolled along, all happy, and chipper. That's when my companion slapped me from my cerebral utopia.

"I can't (expletive deleted) believe our kids may not get to have this river!" she blurted out, out loud. Really loud. She huffed once, gritted her teeth for a moment, then seemed to pull herself together. Quickly it was all over; we went back to looking around in our individual silences.

What she was referring to, of course, was the Animas-La Plata Project – the $700 million water project that will soon divert much of the Animas from this point, pumping it over the nearby range of hills to fill a reservoir presently being built in a big basin west of here. What triggered her outburst was that our route along the bike path had taken us directly across the river from where the water project's massive pumping station and river diversion is to be erected. We had a clear view of it: The site is only twenty yards from the boat launch, just a fly-rod's cast from the fishing trail, a baseball's throw from the visitors center and the big play ground, and immediately downstream from Smelter Rapid.

As we wandered on, my thoughts wandered again, ricocheting from replaying my friend's brief emotional eruption, to other thoughts on ALP, to other thoughts on emotion, to emotional thoughts on ALP....

Something bothered me. It wasn't my friend's anger; I, myself, am prone to spontaneous and sometimes untimely emotional outbursts (when, for example, confronted with acts of greed, waste, stupidity, like ALP). That character trait seems to be the burden of my bleeding-heart, poesy-sniffing, misty-eyed, tree-hugging, pagan-esque disposition and family lineage. But, something still nagged me....

We continued along, moving downstream past the pump-station site, down to the old wood-and-steel auto-converted-to-foot bridge over the river, over what may one day be a forever low-water river. We stopped again to check out the kayakers surfing in Santa Rita Hole, which ALP will reduce to only a legend told around the bar. And while we watched, I pursued that nagging feeling.

And there I found it, lurking behind the obvious. It wasn't my friend's momentary meltdown in fully justified anger that bothered me, I realized, it was what she did after that. What she did represents what many people who share our intangible, unexplainable, gut-level and rooted-in-our-genetic-soil feelings about things like rivers do after those feelings erupt as emotions: We quickly pull ourselves together. We quiet down and chill. We "return to our senses." Sometimes some of us even pull back, embarrassed, like we were the ones who farted at dinner.

There are a lot reasons why many of us who love the river — any river, all rivers, as well as mountains and forests and canyons and wildlife — don't let those feelings and emotions see much light of day or public display, but those reasons usually stem from one root: it is unfashionable to say we love the river. I say unfashionable because, while in the past — I mean the multi-million-year thread of human past, extending beyond our mere ten thousand-or-so years of urban living, extending beyond our one civilized culture that has swept over the earth like bread mould — people saw all the world as living "people." And as "people," they were treated as equals, friends, allies and companions worth loving and defending.

But that's not how rational people talk today in this age of reason and objectivity and utilitarianism and profit-making.

And rational people don't let irrational non-objective emotions enter discussions about harnessing those natural resources for human use — the highest and best use, according to our culture. In the media, public forums, impact studies, and cost/benefit analyses, we must stick to only measurable, quantifiable, rational points, please — economics, engineering, law, and politics. And for making those points, only the experts are qualified; we embarrassingly emotional Neanderthal-like nature-geeks who don't have the degrees or can't mumble the jargon, and instead spout off about love and connection and wildness and our kids' kids, just get that humoring smile and condescending nod.

Leave it to the experts. Follow the rules. Don't embarrass yourself.

Well that's bullshit. I'm setting myself up for some abuse here, but I'll say it: I love this river. I love it for what it is: an unharnessed, wild, free-flowing stream; an artery throbbing with the pulse of the seasonally rhythmic heart of the living San Juan Mountains. I love it and need it like a friend, even like my flesh-and-blood friend here. I need to use the river, but as a friend, as a "person," I am willing to sacrifice to limit my use to employing but not exploiting. I need it to be just what it is, and I need to be part of it as it is.

And I'll say this, too: as immeasurable, unquantifiable, non-objective, a-rational, and unprofitable as these sensibilities are, I know these things matter. They matter as much as — more than — all the tidy numerical projections of acre-feet and dollars and increase in property values and short-term jobs and lawyers' fees and on and on, all the numbers that the experts can spew forth ad nausem. I — *we* — know the other things are just as real. More so, in fact. But because they're immeasurable, unquantifiable, non-objective, a-rational, and unprofitable, they don't compute in the experts' control-and-manage software brains and hard-wired bank-account hearts.

Excuse me. I just kicked my desk.

I can now hear the nervous tittering, even from my fellow environmentalists, many of whom do a fine job fighting for the land we love, even on the accepted terms of economics and resource management. Still, though, in the long run, this angle of attack will not protect the wild places left; for by agreeing that those rational values are the playing field on which the future of the land will be decided, we have from the kickoff given home-field advantage to those who would reduce our living landscapes to mere resources and money-making opportunities.

What would happen, though, if the environmental debate's limits were pushed back to include the other valid values and costs of development — expanded to encompass non-numerical and non-economic relationships to the land, non-human life, and with future generations of people? What if the decision also had to consider those human values?

For example, like what I see right around me here right now. Think about this: The Animas River is the largest remaining free-flowing tributary of the Colorado River. No other major tributary of this river, the West's backbone, is undammed or undiverted. Run down the list from the Colorado's source: the Fraser, the Williams Fork, the Muddy, the Blue, the Roaring Fork, the Gunnison, the Dolores, the Green, the San Juan, the Little Colorado ... All these rivers, all the way down to the Gulf of

California — which the Colorado River does not even reach anymore — are tapped, altered, harnessed, un-wilded. You must back upstream more than 200 river miles from the San Juan's confluence with the Colorado (and that confluence is, of course, under a reservoir) to reach the first still-wild arm of the Colorado River: the Animas River.

Yell it: Enough! (Don't be embarrassed!)

The Animas is, or should be, only a tiny side-stream in the Colorado system's grand fluvial scheme, but instead it is the last living remnant. As such (and, actually, regardless of this) this makes the free-flowing quality of the Animas River a rare and precious treasure worth preserving for future generations. Because of this, the Animas should be the place we show we are capable of some restraint, that we can set some minimal limits, that we have some respect for the river that has given so much to feed and nurture our industrial Western culture. As someone once said, any damned fool can make a reservoir, but only God can make a river.

And ALP destroys more than just a river: It also will submerge the area's finest remaining low-elevation elk and deer winter range when it floods Ridges Basin, close to Durango, yet isolated over a little-visited range of hills south of town. As winter range, Ridges Basin is irreplaceable, providing a 500-strong elk herd not only essential winter forage, but also a safe place off the highways and out of the Animas Valley's growing number of fairways and backyards.

And Ridges Basin was meant to remain there for the animals. Until recently, Ridges Basin was public land, held in public trust for the area's wildlife. That was why a "forever wild" clause was written into the deed when the Bodo family gave their ranch to the Nature Conservancy, which in turn entrusted it to the Colorado Division of Wildlife. "Forever wild," that is, until the Bureau of Reclamation condemned the property, since it was the only way to get around that illogical and unprofitable clause and steal this public land.

So let's face it, here are the real questions in the Animas-La Plata debate: Do we again, as we have done to so much of the West already, sacrifice wildlife and wild country and wild rivers for short-term jobs, golf courses, coal mining (for which ALP's water is headed), and so the developers of subdivisions can offer waterfront property in dry piñon and juniper country?

Scream it: No! (Trust your feelings!)

Or will we expand our society's discussion of things like land and rivers and wildlife and our kid's kids to include the full spectrum of human values?

Stand up and mean it: Yes! (Ignore the rules!)

The sooner we say we value and will not destroy rare and irreplaceable wild remnants like the Animas River, Ridges Basin, and our beloved elk and deer herds, and the sooner we are willing to rally around and stand by the other remaining wild places we love and need – and our great grandkids will need even more – then the sooner we can put that now-wasted brain power, emotional energy, and money into resolving our real issues: there are too many of us using too much of our land and water for green grass and trophy homes and wide, smooth highways for our big, rugged SUVs, and on and on.

To do that, though, those who know those human values of spirit and emotion and restraint and respect must be as willing to speak as the number-experts are, for even if it's out of fashion today, gut feeling is still the knowledge and emotion the jargon of our experts — experts in the multi-million-year-long experience of humans living with the land.

What's really radical about
the Endangered Species Act

I was having a nice dinner with an acquaintance once, when the conversation drifted to the Animas-La Plata Project. At the time, ALP was stalled by the Endangered Species Act, while the agencies involved studied the project's impact on the endangered Colorado pike minnow (then called the Colorado squawfish).

"Can you believe they're not building the Animas-La Plata because of a stupid *squawfish*," my dinner companion blurted out.

I smiled, being a polite sort, and answered gently, "Why, yes, I can."

Some people think this position is radical. Some people think the ability of a little-seen, little-known and nearly extinct fish to block a huge economic-development proposal such as the Animas-La Plata Project is exactly why the Endangered Species Act should be weakened or abolished.

But the only radicalism surrounding the Endangered Species Act is in those who would weaken or abolish it. What's truly radical is the immense, short sighted and greed-driven arrogance that says this one generation of humans has the foresight and right to sentence to extinction a multi-million-year product of evolution.

The Endangered Species Act is an attempt to temper that arrogance. The act says that even though we can build that project (or that power plant or that shopping mall), and even though it may be profitable to do it, sometimes we shouldn't. We shouldn't, the act says, because this generation has obligations and responsibilities to future generations that sometimes outweigh our present economic opportunities.

The Endangered Species Act isn't just some tool of special interest environmental groups, as opponents charge. What makes the act such a brilliant and visionary piece of legislation is that it is the tool of those future generations. The job of the federal government is not just to grease the path of industrial development; it is also the government's role to stand up for the non-economic values of future generations, and that includes making sure some semblance of a functioning wild world is passed on and not disassembled in a few short decades.

When it comes to deciding what kind of world we pass on, it's unfortunate that we need the Endangered Species Act, but we do. When defending the natural world, or individual species in particular, threatened and endangered species and the environmental groups that stand up for them are usually outgunned. The reality is that in many cases only the federal government is strong enough to stand up to the economic steamroller when business doesn't have the moral forbearance or vision to know when to say "enough." The act provides a limit.

When you look at it, the limit imposed by the Endangered Species Act isn't some radical monkey wrench to progress — it is a last-ditch point. In its present form, the Endangered Species Act is as weak as it can be and still work: In order for a species to earn the "endangered" tag, it must be in danger of extinction in all or a significant portion of its range. Also, by definition, species on the Endangered Species list cannot have reached that point by natural events; they are pushed there by development.

Of course, despite what some of the radicals cry, we aren't faced with the do-or-die choice of either sacrificing some species to build more power plants or else being confined to evenings of candlelight perusal of tattered copies of the Mother Earth News (as one critic of the act recently wrote in our local newspaper). The real choice is to either continue sacrificing species to unchecked economic development, or to accept reasonable limits for industrial uses of ecosystems, and at some point to adapt, to put the human ingenuity and technological innovation of which we are so proud to use finding alternative solutions that don't require the deaths of entire species.

Should the Endangered Species Act be changed? Sure. It needs to evolve as we learn from practice about its strengths and weaknesses. As it is now, with its species-specific focus, the act too often allows proposed projects to absorb investment before the projects come up against some species protected by the act, as was the case in the Animas-La Plata Project. To avoid these situations, the Endangered Species Act should evolve into some kind of ecosystem protection act. An act like this would have a pro-active vision of species and habitat protection that would tell developers early on whether a project will endanger threatened species and habitats. That way, from the beginning projects can be designed to minimize harmful impacts, or they can be ditched before too much money is wasted.

Improve the Endangered Species Act, yes. But weaken or abolish the act? No way. The fact is, not all of us are willing to condemn our children's children to a natural world of aquatic tank-raised squawfish and salmon and snail-darters, of textbook pictures of lost species, or to a world in which the only species allowed to live are those that have proven their economic worth.

Many of us want to pass on a whole, intact world. That desire isn't radical, it responsible.

And if some dam project or coal-fired plant or housing development is shot down to save some little-seen, little-known species like the Colorado pike minnow? Then that is a small price to pay to deliver to future generations all the parts of a natural world that is so complex we can't even begin to understand it, and a world we certainly don't have the right to tear apart for the sake of 10 or even 100 years worth of economic gain.

Trail fees take the public
out of public lands

Spring: Endless snow in our mountain home, an overwhelming glacier of work on my desk, and the media a nauseating blizzard of war news.

Time for a run to my personal Mecca: Cedar Mesa, a big, broad, canyon-carved shelf of piñon-juniper forest in southeastern Utah. And all public land, where we are free to put our flesh back in touch with the elements and rekindle some of those primal skills of getting in and out of the backcountry. And not just I need it — Sarah and the kids, too, ache for canyon time.

So imagine our surprise when we pulled up to where the two-track to a favorite canyon had once been, and in its place we find a wide, bladed road with a big BLM sign instructing us to stop and please pay $2 ($8 to camp overnight) for the privilege of walking around out here.

Pay? Yep. The Recreation Fee Demonstration Program has come to the Four Corners, as it has to more than 100 public-land trailheads around the West.

Time to pay to play, folks, if the Forest Service, BLM and a cartel of major recreation-equipment corporations, under the guise of the American Recreation Coalition, has their way. Begun in 1996 (cowardly, as a rider attached to an Interior appropriations bill), the Recreation Fee Demonstration Program allows public-lands managers to institute fees to test the public's acceptance of the fees. Slated to end in 2004, most believe the program will be made permanent before then.

It's only fair, defenders of the program say. Why shouldn't hikers, picnickers, bird watchers, hunters, fishermen, bikers and other daydreamers pay for their use of public lands, like loggers, miners, grazers do?

Why? Because there seems to me to be a big difference between my throwing up a tent and wandering around the slickrock with my kids, and what else I see here on my beloved Cedar Mesa: the big square scars where the BLM has chained the P-J forest bare so grazers can try to grow forage in the desert; the below-cost Forest Service timber sale clearcutting hundreds of acres of aspen to the north of here, on Elk Ridge; the oozy green cowpies I have to step around to read the fine print on the sign.

Fairness? No. There's a shrewder strategy behind the rec-fee demo program: What trail fees do is put those touchy-feely, non-quantifiable values of our public lands on the quantifiable economic playing field. Turn these aesthetic "uses" into paid-for amusements, and they become just more revenue-generating line-items where, at last, the joy of just being outside can be compared numerically alongside all those profit-making consumptive abuses to determine the "best" uses of our public lands.

And guess which will win? Unless, of course, recreation can justify itself by generating more income, through increased fees, or developing profitable industrial tourism, or by adding revenue-generating services ... and the amusement-park cycle is on.

The problem, as I see it, is not that public lands don't pay their own way, the problem is thinking that public lands should have to pay their own way. That's the point of public lands: they are refuges of undeveloped, unprofitable, and unindustrialized land protected from the great cult of economics devouring big open spaces everywhere else.

To many of us, our public lands are an investment in national spiritual-health care: places held in trust so all Americans can afford to get out, away from our ever-more-crowded and commercialized world.

Places our kids will need even more than we do now.

Back on Cedar Mesa, I finish reading the sign and then climb back in the car. We drive on without paying, even though we risk a fine ($50 to $200). As I see it, paying the fee is a vote in favor of it. And besides, I like to be a role model for my kids. We wind and grind our way into the backcountry until we find a hidden spot above our once-hidden canyon, a great grey gash snaking away toward the San Juan River.

The kids climb out of the car and run off, cheering and doing some kind of kiddie jig, shamelessly exploiting their public lands. And I just watch and think: to raise kids right, we need places to raise them right.

And that is the real best use of our public lands.

It's a man-thing, man.

*T*his, I will be the first to admit (but not the only to suggest), may not be the smartest place to be. But here we are.

Where we are is somewhere out in a big, empty, remote section of canyonland desert in the cold heart of winter. We stand in the dark under the heavy overcast of a pre-dawn sky. On the wet clay ground next to the truck, in a spot dug out of a half-foot of fresh snow, a little aluminum pot full of coffee water competes with the granitic cold of December for the heat from a little backpacking stove. My friend Steve and I stare at the little flamethrower. Can't see much else. There's not much else to do.

Not rational. Not politic. Not very comfortable, even, to be here. It's certainly not even "fun," at least in that marketed sense of entertaining and amusing. But we think this is fun, even if it doesn't make sense and we sure ain't doing a damn thing for the economy.

Just ask our wives. They sympathized, even if they couldn't empathize, when Steve and I tried to explain our need to get out here, right away, despite and regardless of an approaching arctic front. For my part, I'm not sure I was successful in offering a satisfactory explanation, but I at least made clear what I did know: It's nothing personal, honey, but I just gotta' go. She knew.

This was evidenced one afternoon when Sarah tried to describe her day to me, soon realizing I was once again staring vacantly through her and toward some topography way beyond the curvature of the earth.

"You haven't heard a word I said, have you?" she checkmated me.

I blinked, attempting to lock my bearings back onto the situation at hand. "I'll do it tomorrow," I smiled warmly, if not correctly.

I know Steve knows this feeling. As we were driving out of town yesterday, I ran down my checklist. "Did you grab some beer?" I asked.

He looked at his wrist. "Yep, it's 2:45."

My wife just says, "I know, it's a man thing." Fortunately. While she may not have understood my compulsion to get out, she understood that I'd be better for it, and, hence, we'd be better for it. So, two days later found me and Steve turning onto a rough, deserted dirt road as the sun set over the Henry Mountains. We finally stopped the car at the crest of a big ridge, where we killed the engine and got out and sat on the hood. We smoked a cigar and drank a beer as the just-past-full moon heaved itself over the desertscape, turning the land spread out before us all silver and shadow. The moon also highlighted, with a soft, unthreatening luminescence, the promised front filling the northeast sky.

"Hey, those weather dudes might be right about that snow," I admitted, puffing on my cigar and, at that point, not caring much.

Steve sat on the hood also smoking away, his ball cap yanked low over his brow, and his jacket collar pulled up like a polyester-pile foxhole against the cold. He grinned big enough to part his mountain-man moustache.

"Even if we had to turn around now, it's worth it already," he said.

We were committed. Or ought to be.

We climbed back into the truck and rumbled and wound farther along the dirt road with just the parking lights on, the back of the car filled with gnarly spiked juniper limbs we had picked up some miles back so we could have a fire on the scrub lands down below.

"You know," Steve said from the darkness across the seat, his arm hanging out the window in the frosty air, glowing cigar roach threatening to ignite his fur-covered lips, "tomorrow they just may find us dead in a twisted mass of metal and wonder why we were driving with just the parking lights on."

"They may not find us 'til spring," I corrected. "And then they'll wonder how we got impaled by a bushel of sticks."

So I ask you: What's up with this? What is this something my body regularly homes in on until its impelling finally overwhelms my reason and I have no choice but to go? What is it that makes me do this kind of silly "man thing" over and over?

Something.

A cowardly response, to just say "something...." But that's not to discredit it just because I can't identify it. Something is there, as real and tangible as sandstone and snow. And I'm drawn to others following this something. We're like a pack a dogs who keep running into each other because our noses are pressed to the ground as we scurry around on the same invisible yet unignorable scent.

Men in general, I think, require regular ventures with men. Nothing new here: It's an argument that's been bantered, debated, defended, and dismissed for generations. Meanwhile, as the discussions of these man-thing men-trips ramble on, the men wander off, to poker nights and bowling leagues and barrooms and drumming sessions and fishing trips and, for some of us, road trips to remote canyons at not-recommended times of year.

I have a theory, though: these various ventures are all the same thing. They're all Astroturf replacements for men's true turf: the bi-weekly or monthly hunting expedition necessary in the hunting-and-gathering tribal life we've spent 99/100ths of our species' time living. What did hunters do on those ventures? Just sit, a lot. Wander around and sniff out intriguing trails. Break routine. Study the surroundings. Be keen and patient and observant. What were the results? Physical challenges. Risks. Adventures. Camaraderie. Shared adventure.

Sounds like a weekend of hunting with my father and his buddies. Sounds like me and my companion here taking off for the canyon country. So it seems to make sense that if we're evolved to be hunters, then we're probably evolved to yearn for those qualities of the hunt.

I can even see this manifesting in my kids. When my six-year-old girl's friends come over, there's a game they play: Lost Little Girls. "We're sisters," the rules always begin, "and our parents died." What do they then do? They make a house; they go out and scrounge leaves, rocks, and bits of wood for food; and then they pass a long, long time preparing it, working diligently side by side, whispering the whole time. Chatting endlessly....

How about Webb, my eight-year-old boy? Driving the other day I asked if it was alright if we took the longer, more scenic back way to our destination. Sarah sighed. She likes to get there. Anna chimed in, "Oh, dad!...." Webb, though, said he'd like to go the long way.

"Why?" Sarah asked him, surprised.

He stared out the window. "So I can have more time to think about cool things."

Oh, yeah.

Boys will be boys? Boys must be boys. And sometimes, men must be boys. Is that the "something" that makes me, and Steve, and my other friends like us do things like come out here in the middle of nowhere in the middle of winter? Not a planned "vacation," but some adventure, gawddammit! A vacation is full of the unknown, sure — breaking routines and seeing some new stuff — but an adventure is about the unknowable. For an adventure to be an adventure it must be unanticipatable, its situations and outcomes plannable only in the sketchiest of ways, and ultimately coming down to just a matter of testing your preparedness and adaptability to the unpredictable unfolding of circumstance. The embracing of chance. Amor fati — love of fate. Like a hunt.

All I know is, I need regular and repeated, almost ritual and religious fixes of the uncontrollable in my life. That blessed, intangible, nonquantifiable, unpriceable something. Something like standing around in six inches of fresh, dry desert snow sipping instant coffee as the day begins to glow enough for the landscape to take on a subtle rusty depth, like an old airbrushed postcard photo.

And that's as bright as this morning's going to get, I think, as the snow resumes.

"Should we head back or stay?" I ask Steve. I know we're staying, of course, but I feel obligated, like a Bureau of Reclamation official at a public hearing on a new dam, to at least give a token semblance of consideration to the opposition.

"Stay," he says, tossing his cold-coffee backwash onto the wet ground.

Okay. No further explanation is necessary. Or possible.

Fear and loathing in the Four Corners

"*R*ide ... the ... snake ..."
I hear Jim Morrison's voice — or a bad impersonation thereof — fly from the bridge and rattle down the canyon. Mark is down a little ways from me, leaning over the rail. I can see his luminescent silhouette in the moonlight.

We're somewhere deep in Utah, and have been descending, physically and morally, since Mancos Hill, 120 or so miles back. Now we're at the bottom of our basin, the heart of our heartland, the core of the canyonlands, on the bridge over Narrow Canyon.

"Ride ... the ... snake ..." Mark sings deeply out toward the slackwater of the flooded canyon, pooled up behind Glen Canyon Dam, some 150 miles downstream, "to ... the ... lake."

I know already, after only three hours on the road, that this trip will more'n likely live up to the lively grandeur of my many other memorable desert ventures with Mark. I never bring a camera on these trips, although we always end up someplace with views that make you alternately run around screaming and then, moments later, bow down and beg forgiveness. No film, though, could capture the views we view and the scenes we see when we're together.

It's not really a camping trip, it's more of a three-day rant. Mark and I don't really converse on these ventures, we just lecture at each other in tag-team intervals, alternating leading pitches as we stalk a polemical route toward whatever landmark idea we began talking toward. It's an exercise in philosophic orienteering.

"It's an awesome landscape," Mark babbles, more to himself than to me, as we sit atop a butte a couple hours later. The full moon highlights the distant line of the Henry Mountains, sprawling spectrally before us like a personal Imax show. Then again, a mountain range is nothing like a movie, and I've come here to remind myself of that.

"Every landscape is awesome, really; the difference is undeveloped landscapes," I retort brilliantly. Game on. "Look how rare this place is: you can actually get 20 miles away from pavement on a dirt road, and then another 20 deeper by foot. We have a treasure here. This is the American Kalahari, but without the hyenas. Except you."

Actually, he looks more like Chewbacca the Wookie at this moment, scrunched forward, his goatee and ponytail hanging there, his face glowing with intent and beer and moonglow.

His turn: "Call it a 'reservation' if you want, but we need places with separate economies. How 'bout a safari economy out here?" – he gestures minister-like toward the dark gaping gorge of the Colorado River — "hard to get into, employing only residents, using only primitive means of getting around. You'd have to really want to be here to come here, or live here, or even visit. But you know what? Fucking Bush is trying to get a few national forests managed with 'private partnerships' with corporations. It's a demonstration program, like the free-demo program. It's the fucking end, man. Your kids aren't going to see public lands."

"It's happening, everywhere," I yell back, "just like my dad saw and told me about back in New England. It's obvious, but what are people doing? We're hiding in our houses, thinking we're activists just because we listen to NPR. Radical today is giving $25 to the Sierra Club and recycling every Wednesday."

And this is why I leave a camping trip with Mark only a pot of coffee and a book of stamps away from Ted Kaczynski.

The next day we walk. Our route is unplanned, unprogrammed, and well off the designated trail that switchbacks down 1,500 feet to the canyon floor. We instead wander for mile after meandering mile along the rim of the canyon gouged below us. How many others walk this slick-rock emptiness? Few. None, probably. Why would they? There's nothing here. Nothing except a ruin tucked and hidden under a shallow overhang ... except a little unappreciated wash that suddenly leaps 800 feet into a vertical-walled sidecanyon ... except broad, rambling drainages and unscalable rimrock barricades and ravens and rabbits and fur-filled coyote scat....

And us. We walk. And, of course, talk, at if not with each other.

In the late afternoon we're stopped on a ledge, sighting in on the butte behind our campsite that we were on top of last night, a couple of miles away. We're discussing possible routes, since there's no trail around to guide us.

"We're so fucking trained," Mark bellows at me, or somewhere in my general direction. "Keep it between the lines! Don't get upset! Jesus, you know what they're doing out at my place? In the HD Mountains, the gas companies want to put 200 new wells in a place that's still basically just a big, low-elevation roadless area! There's not much of that left. And you should see the elk there! And where are they gonna go? The Animas-La Plata Project will flood Ridges Basin, formerly in the Bodo State Wildlife Area, and they're putting 250 new houses in the Animas Valley above Durango. 'Elk Haven' they'll probably call it — a fucking tombstone is what it is."

I'm with you, buddy, I'm thinking. But this year, I'm not as quick with the obituary-list repartee. This year, I'm thinking a little differently somehow. Something's been on my mind, on my soul. Mark's good at this stuff — he's well-read, academically grounded, news-savvy, a politically shrewd and practiced activist. And I used to be able to hang with him. In my midlife, though, I find myself wandering down more pragmatic trails, thinking a bit more closely to home and day-to-day life. I find I'm in more of a karate mentality: What you throw at me out of my reach doesn't concern me, if I can protect what's in my "box" — arm and foot's reach. I've been thinking about my box ...

We pick a line and trust we'll find a way across the washes and up that far canyon wall over there. This is the art of canyoneering: when there's no trail, you need to be patient. Look at the landscape, without expectation or plan, and let a route materialize. Then keep adjusting your plan as you work toward your landmark. Follow the flow of the landscape as it unfolds before you.

So we go, passing through a frozen moment in a liquid landscape. Nothing moves ... yet the landscape is the definition of movement: great white and rust-red blocks of sandstone corroded off the rim hang in the rubble piles below us, paused in their descent ... washes sit dry, waiting to run in torrents ... buttes in the distance stand sloping like half-melted candles ... canyons slice through the bedrock in great knife cuts ... but it's all at a standstill while we stand still, staring.

It seems frozen, but the landscape is liquid. Everything is liquid — "all stream," as Buddha managed to summarize everything in two words. Change — day to day, moment to moment — is the norm in the world, and, therefore, as Bruce Lee says, "Changing with change is the changeless state." What Zen calls the "Original Mind"; and what is Zen, after all, but an attempt — through effort and training — to regain that hunter-gatherers' mind of awareness and presence, free of expectation or clinging, changing with change?

Yet that is the mind our culture endeavors to subdue. Our culture's purpose is to create a completely predictable world in which nothing changes — everything must be mapped, planned, predictable, committed to, and secure. People count on you to be somebody, who you've always been, not become somebody. Even our physical world must be controlled — "We go from our warm houses to our warm cars to our warm workplaces to our warm cars to our warm houses to a cold beer and the goddammed TV!" Mark preaches to the unsympathetic p-j forest.

And that's why lately I've been thinking about my box. And I've noticed that my box seems to be a very nice 2,000-square-foot domicile that offers me a year-round climate, numerous labor-saving devices, an ever-full larder for food I hunted and gathered right where I knew I could (cereal: aisle 2), lots of storage for the many things I seem to keep buying to fill this abundant space, and an endless stream of stimuli that makes me feel like I'm really doing something – music fills my ears, TV satisfies my adventure-yearning mind, and that evening glass(es) of merlot or morning vat of coffee offers a remarkable simulation of the adrenaline I'm not experiencing. And should deeper, genetic, primal urges rise and threaten to disrupt my or others' comfort, well, then, there's always Prozac.

Meanwhile, the daily outside is just what I pass through on my way to the car or the office or what I glimpse while I walk the dog.

But it's that daily outside, that ever-changing world we evolved in, that my senses crave. And that's the philosophical landmark – well off our cultural map – I've been letting a route unfold toward lately. And it has led me across some interesting terrain.

I've been thinking ... Sure, I do some cool things because I live here in the Four Corners, but even though I moved here for the chance for the truly different life this unique place offers, I've let my lifestyle grow indistinguishable from how I'd be living if I still lived in suburban Boston. I've been thinking lately that living differently is not about the scenery or camping trips the Four Corners offers: it should be about daily life – a life of daily change, challenge, and awareness ... a primitive life ... a life alive.

I've been thinking: Could I construct something as close to that primitive lifestyle of extreme – radical, even – simplicity while still being able to function in the "real" world? What could I control to seek a more simple way of living? Could one pull off, say, some kind of Walden by Van, or retreat by tipi?

I've been thinking: Could I walk every day in the mapped world – keep it between the lines! – but every night wander off the trail and melt into the bigger world, out there? Even in the face of the disappearing wilderness and devastated wildness all around, could I regain some of my human wildness – changing with change? Not a lone eagle, but more of a raven. My favorite bird: Ravens are adapted wildness, still following the same genetic software they flew off the glaciers with yet artfully working within the circumstances they find themselves in — that we all find ourselves in these days.

And I've been thinking: Could I show this to my kids? Would this be the greatest gift of parenting — to give my kids real choice, not just of how to make a living (all the choice our culture offers), but a choice of how to live?

This is where my philosophical orienteering has led me. It's finding the actual route there that's the hard part. Meanwhile....

"Did you know that Strontium 90 is in everyone's bones?" Mark spouts as we pull ourselves through a narrow crack in the canyon rim. "That shit didn't even exist until World War II. Did you know Bill Moyers went and got tested for 100 carcinogens? He had every one in his body."

I hear him, but somehow that information is outside my box just now. I'm too busy looking around ... smelling the sweet sage ... feeling the caress of the breeze on my neck ... thinking about bringing my kids here ... waiting for a route through the chaparral ahead to unfold so we can keep moving toward that butte over there in the distance ... and toward that philosophical compass bearing beckoning me.

And I'm thinking ...

The Elders at the Apocalypse

*T*he first time I met Don, I thought he was just a senile old guy. In retrospect, this was a bit rash. But he looked the part, there in the dark at the Green River boat launch in Dinosaur National Monument, standing in his rubber booties, sipping from a can of Busch and grinning like a carved cantaloupe behind magnifying-glass glasses.

This was after the seven-hour shuttle, which followed the six-hour drive from home. I was back in the riverside darkness of camp, groggy and somewhat disembodied from the epic drive, and seeking sleep with the help of a few beers. So I feel I can be forgiven any early assumptions about Don. It would take me the next few days on the river to get to know him better, to really appreciate what, despite our thirty-plus-year age difference, we share, and to grasp what he would come to represent to me.

Of the group with whom my wife and I and our kids (ages 5 and 7) would be spending the next five days, I knew only Bill, a fifty-something year-old lawyer whom we'd met on a river trip last year, and who had invited us on this venture. The rest of the group looked like an AARP outing — Don and his wife, Kathy, were in their 70s; Bill and has friend Kenny were probably in their fifties; and the other two guys, Henry and Jim, were in that same age range, and, from first impression, looked like they could've been paying tourists from Nebraska.

What had we gotten into? I wondered, nodding politely to all and crawling off to my sleeping bag.

It's the first morning on the river, and I feel better about things. After a good sleep, after finally — finally! — getting on the river, there are, for a while at least, no concerns. Our group disperses and floats in our respective boats, drifting in and out of occasional small-talk contact, then bobbing off back into our own spaces. Sarah and I and the kids are happy to be off alone a lot, relishing these first river-trip hours, savoring like foreplay what's ahead of us: five days on the Green River in northwestern Colorado, a new canyon to my family and me, and all that newness implies — new rapids (bigger than anything the kids have yet run), new canyons, new side canyons and riverine campsites.

Excitement. Yet, for me, the excitement is tempered some. Even though I float peaceably through the red-rock beauty of Ladore Canyon, a vague ominousness lingers. Justified? I pick up the book I brought along, the classic Exploration of the Colorado River and its Canyons, and find none other than John Wesley Powell himself knew this foreboding. And it proved justified.

> *We enter the canyon, and until noon find a succession of rapids, over which our boats have to be taken ... A boat riding such billows leaps and plunges along with great velocity. Now, the difficulty in riding over these falls, when no rocks are in the way, is with the first wave at the foot. This will sometimes gather for a moment, heap up higher and higher, and then break back. If the boat strikes it the instant after it breaks, she cuts through, and the mad breaker dashes its spray over the boat and washes overboard all who do not cling tightly ... We have had several such experiences to-day.*

True: This isn't quite the same river Powell encountered. Thanks to the dam corking Flaming Gorge, upstream of the Canyon of Ladore (both of which Powell named), today the Green runs with only those steady, ever chilly, carefully titrated dam-leaked flows so common in the modern West. No doubt, the canyon's rapids — which had earned intimidating, respectful honorifics from Powell, such as Upper and Lower Disaster Falls, Hell's Half Mile, and SOB — can still reach out and whop a boat. But they rarely threaten lives anymore.

Even if the Green is no longer the raging river it once was, we still get our share of excitement when we, too, reach our first "succession of rapids, over which our boats have to be taken.": Upper and Lower Disaster Falls.

Powell named this cataract in tribute to a learning experience:

I pass around a great crag just in time to see the boat strike a rock and, rebounding from the shock, careen and fill its open compartment with water. Two of the men lose their oars; she swings around and is carried down at a rapid rate, broadside on, for a few yards, when, striking amidships on another rock with great force, she is broken quite in two and the men are thrown into the river. But the larger part of the boat floats buoyantly, and they soon seize it, and down the river they drift, past the rocks for a few hundred yards, to a second rapid filled with huge boulders, where the boat strikes again and is dashed to pieces, and the men and fragments are soon carried beyond my sight.

We can relate, sort of.

Upper Disaster Falls is a short shot down a pouroff between a couple of big boulders, on either side of which are steeper, potentially boat-flipping falls. Exciting, but no problem. Lower Disaster Falls — where Powell's men found disaster in June's full-faucet, dam-free runoff flows — is technically more challenging, but even less threatening: a couple-hundred-yard fast-water run through a few thousand big rocks. Aside from some bumps and spins and some grinding over shallow sleepers, the first three boats make it down the run and eddy out at a nice beach below the rapid.

One boat is missing, though. Kathy paddles up to us in her duckie, and it's obvious she's agitated. The other boat is stuck at the top of the rapid she says, and they can't seem to get it off. "They" is Don, Jim, and Bill. Don, by the way, she informs us, is recovering from a recent heart attack. And Bill had quadruple by-pass surgery last year.

What have we gotten into? Kenny and I grab rescue lines and head off along the shore upstream.

The scene looks simple enough: The boat sits high, but it's still in the water, pinned by the current on a big boulder. The boulder sits low enough in the water that the boat remains relatively flat, with no threat of a wrap. The three guys maneuver around inside the raft, trying to alternately push, pull, heave, kick, cajole, lift, heft, and yank the boat back into deeper flows. There are some problems, though. Problem 1: the water around the boat is too deep, cold, and swift to get into to aid this lifting process. And the little 14-footer is sorely overloaded. Problem 2: they are way too far out in the river for Kenny or me to reach or throw lines to them. They're on their own, heart conditions and all.

For more than an hour they labor, rest, try something else, rest more, and try again. They shift gear around, wobbily yanking and swinging heavy bags in the rubber boat. They work together to heave the boat in one direction, then the other. They attempt from different angles to slide the craft off to one side, then give up on that and attack from a tiny perch on an exposed sliver of the rock holding them fast. All this futile exertion is made worse, of course, by the unavoidable awareness that a fall and a swim here would be harrowing — it may not be a tough rapid from the confines of a nice raft, but it would be a big-time cold-water bump-and-grind ride in a lifejacket. If you didn't have a heart condition when you hit the water, you would by the time you got out, a quarter mile or more down the way.

Powell's adventure, by the way, went on for a spell as well. And he, too, sat on the same shoreline debating the merits of various possible rescue options. Powell and his crew managed, with the help of one of Powell's other big wooden dories, to rescue the water-bound men. But Powell mourned the loss of the gear housed in the disaster-stricken boat:

> Down the river half a mile we find that the after cabin of the wrecked boat, with a part of the bottom, ragged and splintered, has floated against a rock and stranded. There are valuable articles in the cabin; but, on examination, we determine that life should not be risked to save them. Of course, the cargo of rations, instruments, and clothing is gone.

Powell lay awake all night fretting over the lost gear, particularly his beloved barometers for determining altitudes since mapping was a key task of his river-tripping mission. The next morning, he determined a try must made to retrieve these essential instruments. Meanwhile, he mused, "The river is rising."

The next day, two of his crew bravely volunteered to give it a shot, taking another of the boats out to the wreck.

> They start, reach it, and out come the barometers! The boys set up a shout, and I join them, pleased that they should be as glad as myself to save the instruments.

Brave men, no doubt. But Powell soon discovered the catalyst behind their bravado:

> When the boats land on our side, I find that the only things saved from the wreck were the barometers, a package of thermometers, and a three-gallon keg of whiskey. The last is what the men were shouting about. They had taken it aboard unknown to me, and now I am glad they did take it, for it will do them good, as they are drenched every day by the melting

snow which runs down from the summits of the Rocky Mountains.

Typical river rats. I know the type.

Back in the present day, after an hour of stalemate, the boat moves. It shudders as the trio stands in the bow on a restacked heap of gear and pull on the stern line. They lean back and yank in unison and the boat inches and edges as they yank again. And again. Then, like a TV show rejoining a program already in progress, the boat returns to the flow of the river, where, like it never stopped following the current, it spins slightly clockwise, resuming its run downstream into the guts of the run through the rocks. Bill jumps to the oars, and Don and Jim frantically grab ahold of some straps.

The boys set up a shout, and I join them.

The flat, umber glow of the setting sun drains up the canyon walls, highlighting the red of the rock and the green of the trees like important passages in a book, until night fills the gorge. Dinner's dish duty is done, and the tired kids are retired, so the adults gather around to share rum drinks, continuing the meeting and greeting process begun around the fire the night before. Already we are bound by the day on the river and the thrills at Disaster Falls, so this social time is cementing work. And celebration. So we drink. We talk. We sit on the sand by the river under the night-light stars.

In the course of the night, I manage to sidle over to Don once again. A great grey-headed and bespectacled jack-o-lantern greets me, his eye-glasses reflecting the fire like two candles. I avoid laughing at the image by querying him about his boat-on-rock experience.

"My life passed before my eyes!" he cackles. The candles in his eyes bob and flicker when he laughs. "You can look at it only so many times, though," he sighs. "You can only pee so much. You finally just gotta go."

He pauses for a moment, glancing off downstream. "It was kinda enjoyable, though," he adds. Then he grins that old-man grin again. But this time that grin looks different. It might be an old grin, but I now see it's a familiar grin. It's that river rat grin — like a secret handshake for us riveristas. It's a grin that says, The river, y'know? Y'never know....

These grins ring the fire. Sarah's eyes meet mine across the flames, and I know we know that even though we don't know these people, after fifteen years on the river we know these people. And in this group, even after fifteen years on the river, we're the newcomers here.

Bill launches into Grand Canyon stories. He'd most recently done it just last summer — 21 days. What really was revving him up, though, was that this time his daughter, age 13, and his 16-year-old son both rowed. Anecdotes and images and renderings of Herculean waves and gigantic swirling hydraulics spill like Bill's drink as he gestures cartoonishly. I can imagine the fire fueling Bill's excitement: It must be all different when those are your kids out there riding those hydraulics. I will learn someday soon. I saw some of it today.

"That's why I asked you guys on this trip," Bills finally says, turning to me and then to Sarah. "My family couldn't come. But ya' gotta have kids on a river trip."

Everyone pitches in their own tales of rivers, camps, flips, swims, and rough runs full of reverence through the maws of great holes. (And I remember an old river guide's joke: How many river rats does it take to change a light bulb? Five. One to change the bulb, and four to sit around and drink beer and talk about what the hole was like.) The flow of river stories rises, flash flooding on the pouring of more cocktails.

I just sit there grinning myself. A bunch of old geezers? Excuse me, I was mistaken. I've stumbled into the camp of a bunch of old-time Four Corners-area river rats. True river rats — life-long, life-time committed river runners — and they've been living like this for ten, twenty years, maybe a quarter of a century longer than Sarah and I have. They've already passed this culture onto their kids. Bill's kids have already rowed the Grand! And Don and Kathy's daughter is a commercial river outfitter in our town.

It's late, but the garrulousness continues. Tin cups and grungy, stained, old plastic coffee mugs are refilled. These are my people, I think, although somewhat blurrily now. Mountain people. River people.

Elderly? No, these are Elders.

The next day, even though the scouting and actual running of rapids comprises only a couple hours of the entire day, they dominate the mood. Even at this low water, the whitewater stretches here in Ladore Canyon are technical, and several are long and need to be scouted. So, when needed, we get out and tromp along through the woods and over ridges, out onto boulders, promontories, and rock bars offering views over the rocky maze we must tackle with oars. The scouting alone is fun, though, and the loose camaraderie sprouted from the story-telling fest last night roots deeper in today's teamwork.

Webb and Anna plod the trails along with us, scouting the rapids like apprentices. We point and talk about where the river augers into boulders, or falls back on itself in a long hole, and where waves would push a boat this way and that. We all walk a little faster than we came as we head back toward the boats.

Load up, grab handholds (or the oars in my case), and hang on. We all hoot and howl down the river.

The kids love it. And for myself, pulling and torquing on the oars, there certainly is an added intensity to it all with the kids in the boat. Rites of passage, for all of us.

At mid-morning we pull up to the scout stop for Hell's Half Mile. Before Flaming Gorge Dam, this was considered one of the great drops in the United States, right up there with some of the Grand Canyon's rapids. Now regulated by the dam, it's gaunt, like a thin skin over a skeleton. Still, as we climb up for a view over the first drop, we agree that you can't ignore the fact a guy was killed here just a week ago. It's still a river.

We scout the drop from some bulldozer-sized blocks of sandstone. Fifteen feet away and below us, the river threads its way through a rock-fall, ending in a narrow falls that explodes against a sharp-edged rock blocking the current. A quick visual analysis of river velocity between the narrow falls and the boulder leads me to conclude there's no way to miss a ride up that rock — the trick will be to crank a hard turn as the river tries to upend us, pirouetting off whichever side of the fang the falls delivers us.

The kids, we agree without debate, will portage.

We sit them on a rock downstream, where the river slows and widens for a short stretch before slipping into the white-water rock garden that is the rest of Hell's Half Mile. We show them where we'll pick them up; we point upstream and diagram where we'll be running and what we'll be (hoping, planning, expecting to be) doing. And we leave them. Sarah and I walk back to the boat. Before we pass out of sight over the scouting rock, we look back: Webb and Anna sit quietly on the little rock in their big orange life jackets, waiting to watch their parents run a gnarly little rapid.

Our run goes as planned — slip behind rock on right, crank with an angle to the right toward the lip of the falls, spin left and push, hard. Hold on while crashing into hole, stabilize boat with oars as needed and able. Ride up rock — we ride left of the knife-edge, then, with the bow over my head, we slide on the pillowing water roiling down the side of the rock.

Then we're out and rowing toward the kids, cheering back and forth to each other.

We set up camp in a thick stand of box elder near a creek that pours over in thin waterfalls from the canyon rim above. Powell stopped here, too, so he could spend an afternoon hiking up that little sidestream all the way to the mesa above. While he was hiking, his men set up camp a short ways downstream, where, like us, they must've enjoyed some aprés-float cocktails from their rescued keg. When Powell finally joined them, he found them fleeing into their boats just ahead of quickly spreading flames engulfing the campsite. More gear was lost — "our plates are gone; our spoons are gone; our knives and forks are gone" — but no problem. "A few tin cups, basins, and a camp kettle; and this is all the mess-kit we now have," Powell writes. "Yet we do just as well as ever." Typical river rats.

We do better than they could imagine. Our crew raises the cocktail flag — a red monkey wrench on a black field — and shares a toast to the day's adventures in adrenaline. We sit around and talk about what the holes were like. Even Webb and Anna sip their Gatorades while they tell and retell their sights of mom and dad riding high on the big rock. River rats in training.

The routine: dinner, dish duty, kids off to the tent, then the rum drinks flow. Again, out come the stories of the Old Runs. A theme appears in the conversation, and it involves things like Flaming Gorge Dam, Glen Canyon Dam, Blue Mesa Dam, Navajo Dam, McPhee Dam. These people, these elders, remember our rivers before dams. They serve up more bygone sagas: the San Juan ... the Dolores ... the Gunnison ... the Colorado ... the Green, now spilling by us in the starlight ... what they were like before.

And my elated mood suddenly stalls, pooling up in a dark eddy. I wonder: Will I one day be sitting around a fire telling my kids about the Dolores (since they now want to dam what's left of it)? Or the Animas River, right down the street from our house, the largest remaining free-flowing tributary of the Colorado, yet in queue to receive the Animas-La Plata Project, "the last of the great Western dams"?

Of course I will be. Is there really any doubt?

I look at the world and see it's a mess, the wild is nearly gone. It's the Apocalypse. It's our personal Ice Age.

But I look around the fire at this tribe — the river rat tribe — and

I look up toward the tent where our next generation of river rats sleep that sound backcountry slumber, and I think ... humans have survived Ice Ages before; in fact, we were forged by them. I look at Don, grinning that happy old man grin, laughing with Bill, the two of them out here still running rivers, damaged tickers and all, and I see another kind of wildness being kept alive. I think of Webb and Anna.

And I think: The world's a mess, but you can only look at it so many times. You can only pee so much. At some point, you gotta say, this is the way it is, and you just gotta go. You gotta just go be wild.

The Monkey Wrench Dad

*I move toward a feeling
that we can make enormous changes,
but that they're not going to be made through change
in ideology, or policies, or programs.
They're going to be made in the way we rear
our children.*

— Paul Shepard

The monkey wrench dad

$\mathcal{S}$ age and sweeping cottonwoods and slickrock ledges and ridges and piñon-and-juniper forest — the fundamental building blocks of southeastern Utah — surround me this morning. I sit with coffee in a tin cup and my face turned toward the chilly morning's rising light.

Gawd, but I needed this.

Still, we nearly hadn't gone that weekend. Forecasters had predicted snow showers around our western Colorado home, and the nights had been very cold, the days still short. So we put it to the kids.

"We want to go camping!" they yelped together.

"But it might be cold."

"Then I'll bring a coat," Anna reasoned.

"And I'll wear a hat," Webb added.

Checkmate. Not that we resisted much. We left that afternoon.

A few hours later we pulled under some cottonwoods off a long dirt two-track in the Utah backcountry. The kids leapt from the car and ran loopy laps around the cottonwoods, into and out of the dry wash, up and down the soft sand of a deep cutbank. The right decision. That night, around a fire after the kids crawled more-than-willingly into their little mummy bags, we laughed at ever having debated the issue.

That was the day before yesterday. Now it is morning and the kids are up; I can see them below me as they eat cereal in their thick sweaters. I sit up on the slickrock slope and look out at the snow-shimmering Abajo Mountains, in their own thick sweater of still-grey aspen stands and girdle of dark spruce and ponderosa. I stood at the top of that range once, about a dozen years ago. Soon it'll be time to pilgrimage up there with the kids.

And that's the kind of stuff I think about as I just sit and sip and sink deeper into the morning.

Until Webb scales his way up the slickrock to my spot. He joins me in the quiet, just sitting and looking, like I am. Imitating me? Or is he really interested in the view? I pull for the latter, but it really doesn't matter — the physical memory is filed nonetheless.

"I don't want to go," he states, unprompted, after a few minutes of shared silence.

I remember again the night before, after dinner, sitting around the fire. We'd spent the day poking up little side canyons and sitting with ruins and climbing around the desert's sculpted bedrock. As we dropped sticks into the blaze and watched them slowly melt into coals, we reminded the kids we'd have to head home the next day.

"No!" Anna barked, then threw an exaggerated glare into the fire — all the supporting reasoning kids sometimes offer for their points of view.

"But we just got here," Webb reminded us. (Which reminded us that "weekends" and "the work week" are not genetically programmed schedules.) "Can't we stay one more day?"

I wished.

"We'll be back again," I reassured him. "A lot."

And I knew it was true, when I looked out over the far ragged, jagged ridgeline glowing dully with moonlight, and upward into the fire-lit cottonwood canopy, just part of a ribbon of cottonwoods running down the valley. We'll be coming back here over and over, I was sure of it.

And still am, I think.

I hope.

I worry.

I worry when I ask myself how long we will really be *able* to come back to this place. I wonder and worry. And I hope Webb and Anna will be able to bring their kids here. But away from the spell of the fire, and extrapolating current trends ahead a quarter century, I get a heartburn that melts into forlorn coals in the face of this grandiose display of public land. What's going to come of this huge, generous swath of space we can now just drive to and park and make a camp and head out on foot in any direction from?

A long sip of coffee.

My most positive yet realistic guess is this will turn into some sternly managed backcountry recreation facility. A federal recreation area, if this land stays in federal — there are already are hiking fees in some of the canyons around here, a symptom of the economic *coup-d'état* attacking our public lands early in the 21st century. And what if that swindling in the name of "revenue" fully succeeds? Then my kids may even see that shady desert grove devolve into a private campground. A state park, at best. Regardless, all visions merge into the same net result: the highest economic return: designated campsites and constructed trails and interpretive points safely fenced and regulated, all to accommodate the weary wayfarers sailing their land-yachts down the smooth highways of the playground Southwest.

Full hookups.

Free HBO.

I see a time when "privateering" makes a comeback with our kids — this time, though, the pirates will be backpackers and hunters and fishers, stealthily practicing their outlawed trades across private and regulated lands.

It shouldn't have to be that way. It doesn't have to be that way. I'm something of an extremist on this topic, but I think it's quite fucking reasonable that our kids should be able to have this, what we have today — a bunch of backcountry, some nice big contiguous chunks of it, to roam around in relative quiet and solitude. Freely. Spontaneously. Like on a Friday afternoon when the family feels like saying, piss on the weather, we're going. And free of charge, permit, reservation, flight plan, appointment, calendar or clock, like humans have been able to do for the last couple million years.

But even without delving into these worst-case scenarios (pictures of mines ... golf courses ... second homes ... the multinational vacation getaway resort and accommodation industry), it doesn't look good.

It's an old story.

It's an old story few retold as well as Ed Abbey, at least as told to those of us under the spell of the American West. And that version of the story was perhaps nowhere better told than in *The Monkey Wrench Gang* — the ribald story of an impromptu gang of saboteurs who, in the name of the freedom of open spaces, turn their despair into dis-repair on the machinery gouging into the Southwest. In fact, Abbey located one of their "night work" projects along Comb Ridge, whose flank Webb and I are sitting on this morning.

The Monkey Wrench Gang was unleashed on the West like a subversive plot 25 years ago. For the next generation of eco-warriors, Abbey's tale became the mythic symbol of their toeing the front line in the face of the march of industrial land-gouging, and the monkey wrench itself became the standard of the radical end of the environmental movement's bell curve. It was the flag around which even this eclectic and anarchistic group could rally.

But 25 years is a long time, plenty of time for movements and their symbols to rise, grow, transform, diversify, then fracture and evolve into new movements. Nothing unusual here, just normal tribal behavior. Just look at the I.W.W., the V for victory, the peace symbol, and the green closed-e of ecology, the fist of black power. Everything has it's time. Look at Earth First!.

So that's why to my friends, I must seem like the old whiskered and whiskery veteran pinning on his faded metals when I don my frayed and faded t-shirt emblazoned with the silver wrench. Or when I slop coffee into the beaten coffee cup with the "Hayduke Lives" sticker plastered on it. Not just friends notice it, either. Anyone can come into my living room and peruse my bookshelves full of dog-eared eco-books, or see the rusty old wooden-handled spanner lying in front of them, or check out the wrench paperweight on my desk. Total strangers, even, can just float by our campsites on river trips and see hanging off an oar a black jack bearing the big, obnoxious red silhouette of the monkey wrench. (My dad made me that flag. How many dads would do that? Not enough. Never enough.)

Dated, maybe, but for me the wrench lives. I still see in it not a passé symbol of a gone-by eco-group, but something way older. Just like *The Monkey Wrench Gang* was another telling of an ancient tale — the land-needing against the land-bleeding — the monkey wrench represents for this particular symbol-making animal, and lots of his friends, attitudes and beliefs rooted somewhere back in the Pleistocene: that we are individually and personally obligated to resist civilization's domestication of the human spirit and the wild landscape, for ourselves and our kids and the land itself, because the latter depends upon the former.

Despite this macho ranting, I, of course, am one of those in the movement who has changed. I no longer find myself so often punching the air at public meetings or getting arrested or practicing much "night work." And when you get down to it, those things are not what Abbey was talking about — not about the programs or the strategies, anyway, and certainly not about any rostered and registered groups or organizations. *The Monkey Wrench Gang* was about spirit. Remember: *The Monkey Wrench Gang* was funny. It was *fun*. It was about appreciating *and* defending. Which is what a lot of people — both those who liked it and didn't like it, both now and when it came out — overlooked. They saw the monkey wrenching, but missed the point: That book was *alive*.

Reread it: It still is.

Living well is the best revenge, Abbey liked to say, but there is no one definition of what "well" means; only your very own personal cosmos-issued conscience can answer that for you, and that answer is different for everyone. Regardless of what it tells you, "living well" means staying on the compass bearing of your conscience, wherever that leads you, and in spite of what the culture, or even the law, sometimes suggests, teaches, urges, reinforces, rewards, requires, seduces, cajoles, or commands you to do.

Living well *is* monkey wrenching.

That same old story, told again.

And told to me, sitting here on this slab of warming sandstone and savoring the last sip of coffee from my monkey wrench-adorned mug as the sun finally erupts over the far ridge and spills on me and my little boy. Yeah, I've changed as I've aged, but the spirit's the same. It's gotta be. My kids are counting on it.

The same old human story.

A river runs through us

*I*n my midlife, I have at last accepted that I didn't miss the boat, it just turned out to be a canoe.

I am bestowed this insight while a couple of friends and I coast our canoes on the slow slide of the San Juan River, in southeastern Utah, wandering around islands and through brush-and-rock country. It is autumn, and the river is a golden cottonwood ribbon through an already winter-brown landscape. We slowly spin under occasional curtains of sandstone, outcroppings of bedrock foreshadowing the canyonlands downstream.

If you shoveled into the compost pile of my life, you'd find canoes decomposing down there, fertilizing the person I am today. All those boats, all those rivers and lakes (and what is a lake, but a really, really slow river?) — I feel them all cycling and recycling when I paddle, an act as innately comfortable and soothing and natural to me as walking to a hiker, as drinking to a barfly, as shaking hands to a politician. It's like I was evolved for it. Maybe so: How deep and old is that compost pile? It's certainly life-long, having grown up on the shore of a lake in southern New England — my primary playmate until I got my driver's license. Ancestral, even, given my family tree (a sugar maple, I believe) — its sap laced with genetic memories of birchbark canoes paddled across wide Canadian lakes and down lazy Northeastern coastal rivers.

Whatever the source, a canoe feels as much a part of me as my right arm. Fortunately for me, my friends get it when I babble on like this.

I'm out here this weekend with Scott — tall, wild-haired, lantern-eyed, and also hardwired to a paddle. He's from Canada, so that explains a lot. He's the embodiment of that Northcountry calmness that is often mistaken for indifference or indolence, but is really some sort of native subarctic Zen.

I remember the time I drove him, his wife, and their two kids to the airport for a flight to Canada. For the 11:05 a.m. flight he asked me to pick them up at 10:45.

"But it's a 15-minute drive to the airport," I observed with an affected calm I didn't really feel.

"Oh," he said, looking surprised I was surprised. "You think we should leave earlier?"

"Yes, I think," I answered again. When I have to catch a flight, I'm one of those who checks in and is sitting in the terminal before the flight crew is out of bed. I convinced him to let me pick them up at 10:30. No matter, of course. We stood around waiting until 10:50.

"Ayla had to run to the grocery store," he explained offhandedly.

"The grocery store?" I squeaked, agitated. "You're going away for two weeks, what the hell do you need?"

He shrugged, as unconcerned as the Rain Man, and just stood there in his driveway blissfully admiring the morning while I paced like an expectant father.

We finally left, me driving like a New York cabbie after a couple quarts of coffee. Halfway there — I swear I was expecting this — Scott suddenly blurted, "Uh! I forgot my green card. Ha!" I glared at him sideways, not daring to slow down even to the speed limit. He must have been able to see my thoughts through my cue-ball eyeballs. "Well...." he offered thoughtfully, "how about you find it and mail it to me, eh?"

Okay, I said. Where is it?

"Well, I'm not exactly sure...."

That's Scott: pure gut feeling and immediate reaction tempered only in the most basic ways by reason. While I think a little anxiety, caution, and planning can be good things sometimes, by watching him I am working on letting myself float through life a little more casually. But it is work for me — it seems my New England Puritan angst is rusted into place.

As for Steve, the other member of our river trio, he knows that Puritan mentality. He's from my home turf, born and raised only 25 miles from my hometown, even though we met 2,000 miles away from there. Steve, too, is an old river runner, another old salt. (Or, since he was a San Juan River guide, does that make him "an old silt"?)

In this group, Scott is the yin and Steve the yang (which may explain why my mother always said I hang out with a bunch of yingyangs). Like me he is occasionally provoked by life's events into bouts of sadness, anger, annoyance, and self-doubt. But Steve has one dominant, redeeming characteristic: he is impeccably honest. Innocently, unflinchingly, reflexively, incontrovertibly honest. "The man is incapable of lying," my wife is fond of saying. And for this he is never unhappy; Steve is always up, even when he's down. But how can you be anything else when everything you do is honest, is only what you *can* do?

I am lucky to have friends such as this flowing through my life. I am lucky to have paddling companions like these. So to celebrate (one can never have too many reasons to celebrate) we carabiner our canoes together and open beers and sodas, toasting over Scott's boat in the middle. As we drift, we spy a few autumn-thin Navajo cattle casting us their vacant, resigned stares from the willows. The river sweeps us along, leaving a wake of cottonwood stands, like it can't wait to get to the real riverworks west of here.

Scott reads his soda can between sips.

"Hey, it says here I can win a one-karat diamond if there's a message in the bottom of my pop can. It also says, 'chances of winning: one in three million'."

"You have a better chance of dying tomorrow," Steve laughs.

Scott thinks about that for minute, sipping his soda and trying to peer down through the clear carbonated syrup. He's not a winner.

"That's good," he finally says. "It should be easier to die than win a diamond in a pop can."

And so goes our impractical bobbing on down the river.

For myself, this is my eighth time down this river this year, on trips ranging from three to ten days. The numbers are about the same for Steve and Scott, and our families. When our kids grow up, they'll think of the San Juan River — its fine-sand beaches, its always-muddy water, its great stands of cottonwoods — as their summer camp. And they'll think of each other, of our families and our time together on the river. They'll think of our tribe, bound by the river.

We stop a few times to poke around some river-side rock houses and stone granaries, ancient and abandoned but still tucked into alcoves and overhangs along the river and up sidecanyons. Across cliff faces scroll long panels of rock art — corn people, snake lightning, Bighorn sheep, and the ever-present mysterious spirals (ancient people all over the world knew what physicists are just now figuring out: that the eddy is the dominant form in the universe).

The deciphering of these psychedelic inscriptions is all speculative, of course, but ... I dunno, maybe I'm missing something complicated, but I look around at the river, with its cottonwood border and the ridges and draws in the distance, and then look back at the glyphs, and ... I get'em. They say the same thing another old friend of mine from the river tribe — "Mad" Roger, who taught me how to guide Colorado's mad high-country whitewater — used to like to say: "It's a kickass world we live in."

In the mid-afternoon we stop at The Cottonwood Site, our name for a campsite under a stand of mammoth grandfather cottonwoods, bent and twisted and in places crawling across the ground and then curling up like gnarly leafed fingers. Above and behind the camp, rising over the brittle-bush and cactus, stands the first rise in the long rock wave of Comb Ridge.

We stop for lunch, and then we strip off our sandals and head bare-foot up the ridge. Barefoot? Absolutely. Call it a tribal ritual. It's something 8 year olds know: there is a direct correlation between the state of your soul and the toughness of your soles. I trot quickly but carefully, leaping cacti and stones, sprinting across a flat, then finally padding up the sandstone slope. We ascend the great 600-foot sandstone sabertooth fang, first walking, then leaning, then all-fouring it up the upthrust of bent bedrock. I climb steadily and quickly, the balls of my feet reading rock, toes grabbing grainy stone. We reach the top in half an hour, converging on the southernmost ridge point.

There we collect our reward: The river is strung out to the left of us, wide behind us, and disappearing off into islands and cottonwoods downstream. Our canoes are three colorful sticks stuck on shore. Directly below and in front of us is a vertical drop to the big valley that runs perpendicular to the river. This drainage, straight as a line of latitude and heading off in the distance to the north, marks the fault line at the foot of this fracture in the land we stand at the tip of. Or one tip of: to the right we can see our perch is the last crest in a line of rock rolling away toward the distant-brown alpine-island of the Sierra Abajo.

What a place, I sigh.

My place.

Our place.

I remember just a few weeks ago ... on a warm autumn morning, my family and I floated the Animas River. Sarah and I each paddled a canoe, each with one of our kids, as we passed the day lolling down the meandering four-hour flat-water stretch above town. There the river is a long, slow ride down the Animas Valley, through big sweeping meanders the river cuts into ranchland meadows. Enormous cottonwoods cast leafy awnings over the water, and roots and deadfalls reach out from shore. Above and behind all this stand the valley's red-striped walls, and above and behind all that rise the ragged headwater peaks of the San Juan Mountains.

Their place. As we went, we pieced together the kids' world for them: over there's the road we hitchhiked on the day my truck broke down. ("Listen you guys," I had crouched down to tell them next to the dead machine. "We're going to put out our thumbs and a stranger will pick us up and bring us home." That generated some open-mouthed stares.

But nothing like the looks I got when it worked.) Now we're under the big rockslide. And over there, across the valley and between those trees, is the waterfall — see it? And back there's the hot spring ... and up ahead is Animas City Mountain, and the rock we stood out on for our Christmas card picture last year....

My wife and I worked on our kids' mental maps until we pulled the canoes from the water, only a few blocks from our doorstep. And why do we do this? Because already they can look up the valley and see the freshly-snowed peaks, and they know that's where the Animas River starts; because the kids have stood on the same slickrock ridge I stand on today, knowing that below them is the San Juan River, and that even though we're more than a hundred miles from home, they know that this is where their neighborhood river ends up.

We're not trying to push any weird ideas on our kids, we just want them to know they live in a valley, not just a town. We want them to be able to feel that difference, because that's when a place becomes a *Place*.

Fortunately for us, and them, and all of us, we have friends who think the same way. A tribe of like-minded thinkers, of like-spirited feelers.

"Hey, let's head down, eh?" Scott finally says, breaking the ridge-top spell I've been under. "I feel like playing some catch." Yes, it's true: we've brought baseball gloves on the river — sandbar baseball is yet another one of our peculiar river-tribe rituals. And as we lope off barefoot down the steep sandstone slope toward our silty leather baseball gloves, I again know I'm fortunate to have friends like this.

Cast away: fishing for meaning
in a tackle box

I first learned of the power of prayer from the most unlikely of places: my father. While my mother had me bowing my head in the pews every Sunday morning, every Saturday my father had me sitting in a boat on a lake, praying for fish. Those prayers were always answered, although not always, or even often, with fat fish.

Let's face it, aside from catching that occasional lunker, fishing is boring. It's absurdly repetitive, and in terms of practical rewards — fish for dinner, or even the excitement of reeling in a honkin' big fish — it gives a pretty poor return on the money and time invested. It's neither practical hobby nor dynamic form of entertainment (and it's also nearly devoid of meaningful exercise, unless you need to train to spin a lot of little handles or jerk a lot of rods). Yet fishing's dullness and numbing repetition are precisely its magic.

Unlike any kind of real "sport," which it decidedly is not, fishing is really more akin to a Buddhist monk's "boom" — a 110,000-time repetition of a simple sacred act, such as bowing, walking around a prayer wheel, or, commonly, dropping from a standing position to prostrating oneself on the floor, over and over again. The point of a "boom" is the intense meditation found in the grueling re-repeating of the act. The reward (as I understand it, although I personally have never "boomed") is the far-beyond-thinking attention one needs to make it the full 100,000-plus cycle, and which leads ultimately to enlightenment.

Fishing is 110,000 prostrations by casting. Personally, though, I find it suits my personality better than dropping to the floor on my chest all day for three and half months. (Not that there's anything wrong with that.) I also like being out of doors in lovely places, and I like being near water. I also really, really like being in boats, especially canoes. And I also happen to love to eat fish.

And, yes, I do like meditation — the practice at just being here, now, in the moment, and the concerted effort at honest and extended personal introspection and reflection. The problem with me and meditation, though, is I've always been way too antsy to feel comfortable just meditating on a pillow in some room. I have too much of the New England Puritan work ethic drilled into me to not feel guilty sitting on my arse. Fortunately, I don't need to. I'm a fisherman.

Yet despite its meditative qualities, strikes from those big fish — like finding enlightenment or having your prayers answered — are less than common. Given the relative rarity of those hits, then, I like mine big and splashy when they come. That's why my all-time favorite kind of fishing is bass fishing on a Northern lake with surface lures.

Some background: I am a devout spincaster, even though all my fishing friends seem to be fly fishermen. This is an unusual relationship, really. Among fly fishermen — especially dry-fly fishermen, the most fundamentalist of the evangelicals — spin fishermen rise a mere earthworm's height off the basement floor, above only bait fishermen in the casting caste system. Despite those fly-fakers's admittedly challenging form of fishing, I am not to be outdone in my own prostrations toward fishing enlightenment.

I make up for their evangelical fervor with my own self-imposed aestheticism. I am an *ultralight* spin fisherman. This means I use a short, thin, flexible, light-weight rod with a miniature open-faced reel hanging from the little handle. I cast only six-pound test line, so playing even a small bass or trout requires careful use of the drag setting and rod. To further complicate matters, I allow myself the service of only a very few lures.

For surface lures, I rely on only Jitterbugs or Hula Poppers. Both plugs' actions are meant to imitate frogs: the Jitterbug rattles back and forth, slapping the water on each side; the Hula Popper you jerk with the rod so it pops the water with its big, flat face. For trout, I'm even stricter: I use only one kind of lure, and in only one color scheme and pattern, varying only the weight of the plug.

I do this for a reason: These restrictions mean that improving my fishing requires more thinking. It requires a better understanding of the lay of the lakeshore or river bottom. It requires improving my fishing through better technique, casting skill, fish handling, and prey analysis. In a nutshell, I'm a spin-fishing aesthete because it's more of a challenge, hence more interesting, hence more meditative. And I believe, even if I am just a lowly spincaster, I am somehow a better person for it.

And when a largemouth bass snags my Jitterbug sloshing across the glassy surface of a darkening evening cove, the water explodes like a depth charge and the rod jumps like it was hit by lightning. Then my frugalness is worth it: that luminescent, tangible flash of a moment suddenly fills my senses. It's a moment whose energy is graspable, fully savorable, only by a razor-edge mind sharpened by the intense, dedicated meditation that 110,000 unsuccessful casts give.

Boom!

Those moments pack whatever punch there is in the "sport" of fishing — and those are the moments glorified in the tackle ads and article photos in fishing magazines. Still, those moments are rare. When sold by volume rather than weight, fishing is the 110,000 casts rather than that one big hit. Yet still I go. Hell, I even ice fish by choice (which means I meet Wisconsin's residency requirement). The fish aside, then, here's really why I fish:

It's a summer evening on a lake in the remote Upper Peninsula of Michigan. I'm alone in a canoe, casting a chuttering yellow Jitterbug toward a stand of white-bellied birch overhanging the shore like mastodon ribs. As I reel, I look up. The sky begins to get chinks in its armor — slots and leads appear in the overcast, and cool blue sky begins to run between bergs of clouds.

By dusk, a half hour later, the sky is burnished aluminum and with a few torn and dying scraps of cloud floating directly overhead. I rest the fishing rod and paddle slowly along the shoreline, slipping along silently and deliberately, keeping a few canoe-lengths off the shore. The air is moist and viscous; I reach and pull myself through it. The paddle drags the canoe through furrows in the liquid earth.

I lay the paddle aside and pick up my little fishing pole to throw a line to the indifferent and unseen fish. I make casts, then listen to the popping of the Jitterbug beckoning the cautious and critical bass I pray are there. But I don't really care that much. As night deepens, the sky fully disrobes and reveals the depth of the stars above the rise of a full and gleaming moon. It's cool, and the Northern sky is sharp and hardedged, like the thin-air clarity of a high-country sky. The voice of a loon flames from the silence, from somewhere down the lake ... loooooooooooHHHHHnnn.... then again the silence is patient and slick, ready to fire a whisper across the lake. I cast ... sit ... casting ... think ... cast ... look around ... make another cast ... do more thinking ...

Then I'm bored of thinking, and I move into whatever perception is beyond that, into no-thinking — just smelling, listening, feeling ... then another cast.

And *that* is why this summer I am following my father's lead and am teaching my own kids to fish. Granted, although pretending to be a frog may not be a very glamorous path to spiritual insight, I want my kids to fish because I want them to sit, and think, and not think, and to just look around, for a long time. I can't help but wonder about the gazillion kids in this country today who never have to be bored, thanks to a free-hand at TVs and videos games and computers, or thanks to the schedules full of structured sports, tutored practices, and chaperoned day-care crowds. What do those kids think about? How do they get to know themselves? How often do they appreciate what's around them? I think kids — like all people — are bettered by reflecting on their selves and their lives. I believe even kids can be awakened to life by getting to practice just ... being ... here ... now.

Yes, I want my kids to meditate — but say that and people think you're some kind of New Age geek. Say that to the kids, and even they will think their dad is some kind of New Age geek. The best part of fishing, then, is I can get them to meditate without saying things like "now we're going to sit in silence for the afternoon," or "children, we're going to spend the summer doing 110,000 bows to the rising sun." Instead, I can lure them in like an alluring Hula Popper with, "Yea! We're going *fishing*, kids!"

The thing that's been amazing me, though, is that the kids seem to *enjoy* fishing. Even when it's boring, as it usually is. And those occasional strikes and fights, and that fresh fish for dinner, well, that's just gravy.

All in all, this is probably way overanalyzing fishing. It's just fishing, after all. Which is not necessarily a bad thing. When a Zen master was once asked what enlightenment was like, he answered, "Do the dishes." He could've said, "Catch a bass."

Call me a Sagebrush Patriot

I live in a fantastic corner of the American West, on the edge of where mountains fall away into canyon-carved desert. I live in one of this area's mountain valleys, but at mid-morning on this day, I find myself on a high above-tree-line pass, taking in a grand sweep of the country. To the east stands a far-ranging range of peaks, rippling away like the choppy surface of a lake. To my immediate south rises a single, massive peak, a great, banded pyramid off whose face falls a sloping scree field that sprawls down and away to the rolling foothill forest lands that reach outward and downward through climate zones, from subalpine fir to piñon and juniper, across the rising and falling of foothills and gathering creeks, then across a river and its side canyons to the green valley bottom where squats the nearest town to the west.

Looking in that direction from this 11,000-plus-foot perch, I can see across dry sage lands for a hundred miles or more, and in that distance I see the wall of a flat table-top mountain, the blue bodies of three distant mountain ranges, and the dendritic arms of two major river systems.

And when I take all this in, I feel lucky. Blessed, even.

Let's face it: we in the American West are blessed. No need to be shy or humble or coy about this. We know it. *We are blessed.*

Sure, sure, there are mountain ranges and deserts and valleys in other places, some really pretty ones, even. But what makes the American West a place like no other, is that, even though this landscape spread out before me today is not all pristine wilderness, the fact remains that much of the American West is largely undeveloped, unindustrialized, and unprofitable. It is inhabited mainly by small, scattered, struggling villages and towns, places where making a living is a constant challenge and is usually somehow tied to the surrounding land, from ranching to mining to tourism. Hard places to get ahead, if that's your aim. But that's okay with most of us who live here because we are strange by modern standards: We like it that way.

For us, the reward for that struggling is all around, all that glorious land we are free to gaze into, to roam over, to work and play on. In the American West, ski bums and grunge rock climbers and line cook/river guides and over-educated, urban-ex-patriot, former-professional manual laborers are the 21st Century pastoralists, joining ranchers and hardrock miners and 1960s back-to-the-earth neo-hunters and gatherers — as well as the earlier, true hunters and gatherers — clinging voluntarily to inefficient and uneconomical lifestyles that view life and land as more valuable than money. We do that because here remains huge expanses of open countryside that are open to all, and built upon this land thrives an intact and interwoven network of working rural communities still dependent upon and humbled by this great landscape.

What is truly blessed about the American West, though, is that, like few places on earth, our kids have a chance to inherit this land-loving culture, to raise their own families amidst big, healthy hunks of wild and rural country that they, too, will be free to wander and work in when they want and need.

It's not by some lucky quirk of fate that the American West remains so undeveloped while the rest of rest of rural American is being bulldozed by people, houses, industry, agribusiness, resource liquidation, repeatedly redundant commercial strips, and sterile suburban mausoleums. It's because we have a defense mechanism, an antibody to the economic-land-development virus, that is also unique in the whole world: public land. Lots of public land. A massive shield of public land. More than half the land between the Sierra Nevada and the Front Range is owned by all Americans regardless of income or residence or social class. And it is this public land that inoculates much of the West from the early 21st Century cult of economics that devours wildlands and guts rural landscapes everywhere else.

Our public lands are the American West — not just the physical West, but the cultural and psychological West. The West's great open spaces — high country, deserts, forests, rivers — give rise to the distinctly Western attitude and spirit we here so treasure, whether we be ranchers or bow hunters or ski bums or bankers. And those great open spaces remain open and accessible because they are public. Yet, remarkably, it seems few people here recognize this bedrock importance of our public lands. Sure, we use them, we hunt and fish and go four-wheeling on them. We go camping and take pictures and enjoy the views they preserve and protect. Some folks who live outside the region just visit them once every year or ten, and then spend the time between visits dreaming and reading and telling stories about them.

And whether we live here or not, we often argue, often vehemently, over how they're managed. But while we argue about the economics and ecology of the uses of our public lands, rarely do we stop to acknowledge that the reason we still have anything to argue about is because so much of this land is public. Without public lands, our arguments would be irrelevant, sold off for subdivisions, strip malls, strip mines, clear cuts, dude ranches, theme parks and façade resorts and posted "no trespassing" getaway homes and gated communities and private game ranches. Need proof? Remember those places that were until recently still rural: New England, Upper Peninsula of Michigan, the Piedmont of the Carolinas, the southern Appalachians.

Yes, we are blessed. But I worry.

I worry because too many of us who do love the West are smugly content to go out and herd cattle or cut timber or bike or fish or hunt or ski or bike or hike while not lifting one tired finger or raspy voice or bloody-knuckled fist to defend the lands that make that work and play possible. I worry because we're all too friggin' busy attacking each other for what the other is doing on our public lands to see that the reason we have anything to argue about at all is because so much of this land is public. But we can't afford to bicker anymore. Once we lose our public lands — all or some, ecologically or economically — they are gone for good.

If you love the West as a holdout of rural communities surrounded by a dazzling and undeveloped landscape that you and your children and their children all own, then you must have the courage to — the responsibility to — stand up. We need to put our arguments aside and rally together over our public lands as refuges not just of land, but of culture. All of us who love and need what these lands give us beyond the dollars they're worth must make a vow: We will not let anyone take them away.

Those who wanted to take these lands away once called themselves Sagebrush Rebels, rebelling against the "public" in public land for the money that could be extracted by making them private. Call me a Sagebrush Patriot: a fighter standing by my country — as in countryside, as in country living, as in big open wild country — where our wild spirits can grow and live, and where our kids can grow up to be both wilderness nuts and ranchers, living and working close to the land, like humans are supposed to.

To do that, we need an army of Sagebrush Patriots, a diverse but unified force of Western people — not just organized environmentalists, but fishermen and hunters and ORVers, alongside backpackers and mountain bikers and loggers and ranchers — standing together as a vanguard for the future.

Blessed people in a blessed country. Let's keep it that way.

Thinking (and sleeping) outside The Box

Here's the scene: I sit in the open doorway of my van's sliding side door. Before me, for my amusement, the moon hangs over the dark ridge like a great glowing banana. It's waxing, a few days past new, and it gives off a dull but definite light that just barely sets aglow the snowy landscape.

Overhead the Milky Way lays across the sky like God's spilled milk. All around me, darkness. A semi-luminescent ridgeline runs nearby, fading off in the distance. A heavy January cold presses on my thick coat. Powwow music from the reservation town nearby beats out of my little pocket radio. After a while, some coyotes start yipping somewhere along the unseeable edges of the basin. And I'm just ... here. Now.

Now isn't this scene the soul of the Four Corners? Isn't this place the essence of this *Place*?

What's especially amazing and fantastic is that this place is just ten minutes from my house. From lots of people's houses, in fact, since I live in downtown Durango.

This is Ridges Basin — so incredibly close to what passes for a major urban area in the Four Corners, yet also remarkably little known. I've always liked to come up here for random visits, walks, drives, and pull-over-and-just-sits. But since I've gotten this big old van, it's become one of my favorite places to park and write and sleep for the night. Lately, this has been just about every night.

I consider this hospice service for a friend. Ridges Basin, of course, is on death row, soon to be submerged by the Animas-La Plata Project. This is an absolute travesty. Yet, as much of a near-town treasure and soon-to-be tragedy as it is, I don't see many other people out here, taking it in while it's still here, savoring the wildness just over Smelter Mountain, listening to the elk and coyotes, saying a prayer for divine intervention. Saying goodbye.

Well, somebody's gotta' do it. So it may as well be me. Besides: It fits in nicely with my Project, which is also how I got the van.

The project that got me sleeping in a van in Ridges Basin began with a simple observation: We don't live in the Stone Age any more. This, of course, is no great intellectual feat. But it led to an interesting question: What age, then, do we live in?

The standard answer that's marketed to us these days is that we live in the "Information Age." But, let's face it, for most people daily life is still largely comprised of manual and/or menial labor — working with nothing so ethereal as "information." So what, then, does define our era? What aspect of our culture is so dominant that it dictates our worldview? What today drives our lives and lifestyles as much as the practical reality of "stone" or "bronze" once did?

I mulled on this for a long time. Then, one lovely day last Fall while I was piddling around the house mindlessly hammering away at some of the many chores this modern lifestyle of ours requires, it came to me: We live in the Home Age.

Look at it: We live in, by far, the biggest, most elaborate, most crap-filled houses in human history. And because of that fact, for the first time in human history our houses rule our lives. They define our lifestyles, encompass our physical world, and encase our most important experiences. We spend most of our time earning money for and maintaining Our Great Big Boxes, and much of the rest of the time we spend inside those Boxes. Our houses are our primary environments and most intimate landscapes: our source of entertainment, food, sensual stimulation, and learning about the world-at-large, all things that used to be done in the wild, natural, changing, challenging, enormous, living world out there.

Welcome to the Home Age.

My problem is I cannot resist The Box. Give me TV, music, climate control, food in the pantry, a beer or three, a machine that washes my dishes, a hot shower at my command ... and I'm in. In what? Inside the goddamned house to much, is what I am. Meanwhile, something inside my genetic code is yelling at me: *People aren't supposed to own more shit than can fit in a tipi, igloo, pit house, wicciup, or grass hut!*

Well, you can imagine the kind of discomfort this sudden insight can cause. Okay, well, maybe you can't. But, trust me, for me it was troubling. So once I saw this picture, I immediately began to look for cracks in The Box that might let in some fresh air and light. And I found them ... around 8 or 9 p.m. most every night. And this gave me the idea for a project. For The Project.

The Project, in a nutshell, is this: Given that I am a father, husband, and homeowner with a full-time job, what can I still do to tip my lifestyle in the direction of nomadic tipi-dweller? What would that change, even small change, do to me?

Well ... as projects do, The Project grew. What began as sleeping out on the deck of our house in August became forays from the back of my car into the hills around town in the fall. And as winter set in, that evolved into a full-blown office-on-wheels — the acquisition of a cheap old van. Or, in the spirit of this adventure, what I prefer to think of as "my tin tipi."

The van gives me all I need, even in the cold heart of winter: minimal shelter, a ready bed, and a place to whip out my laptop and put in a few hours of writing every night — which is what I used to do at home anyway, when I could drag my slothful ass away from baseball, ER, or the History

Channel. With the van, I can get a walk and my writing in at night, and then wake up to the La Platas, or the Animas River, or the woods, or the majesty of Ridges Basin right out my sliding door.

I get what that archaic blood in me whines for: daily doses of variety, mobility, fresh air, cold, the phases of the moon, solitude, challenge, change, awareness, and sensuousness. And then: it's home to get the kids off to school, and myself off to work. And all day, I'm wondering what that night will be like, or what landscape will greet me in the morning.

Not everybody understands this. Let's face it, it just ain't normal. Like, for example, the deputy who came by my first night out in Ridges Basin. He pulled up while I was sitting in the doorway of the van in the dark. There must be a police profile for suspicious parka-clad middle-aged men parked in old vans in the middle of nowhere, because while shining his big flashlight around he launched into the standard probing questions: What are you doing? (Just hanging out enjoying Ridges Basin while it's still here.) Are you camping here? (Yup.) When will you be leaving? (In the morning. I have to get my kids to school and go to work.)

He didn't seem to quite know what to make of those answers. He wore a frustrated look like I had to be doing something wrong. Then he gave up and left. Minutes later the elk were cow-talking again, and the moon sank solemnly into the west.

Who does get it? Some of my more peculiar friends (who will remain nameless, to protect the guilty); my wife, maybe, sometimes, but who, above and beyond the call of duty, puts up with my strange callings; the coyotes who still make a living running around Ridges Basin (one lovely full-moon evening I pulled into my parking spot, jumped from the cab, and in a moment of spontaneous joy, let out a loud howl into the starlit night; seconds later from across the basin came a responding chorus of yipping and hooting); and, most pleasantly surprising, my son gets it.

Webb is only 9 years old, but I'm beginning to think he, too, may be a carrier of the Neanderthal Gene that plagues my family. I remember early in The Project, when I was still just sleeping out on the little second-floor deck that is outside his bedroom, he began joining me out there. After a while, Webb started heading out there by himself while I was downstairs writing or watching TV. He'd lie in his sleeping bag with his Petzl lamp glowing on his forehead and read Harry Potter or SI For Kids, then fall asleep under the big blue spruce that hangs over the porch.

He was a bit more reluctant to join me in the van, but that, too, changed once he came. When we arrived in the basin his first night out, the first thing we did was go for a walk. We pulled on our big coats and hats and gloves and headed down the dirt road under the stars. Soon his grumbling turned to wondering: Is that the Milky Way? Wow! Look at Orion! You can see his whole bow! Where's the North Star? Then he asked questions about why I was camping out every night, and what I'm writing about these days. Then he started telling me stories about things that happened in school, when at home he usually just says "nothing."

Back in the van, he crawled into his sleeping bag while I pulled out my laptop. He lay there reading with his headlamp. Then he rolled over and looked at me and said, "Dad, this is so cool." He has joined me at least once a week since.

Let's face it: kids just get it. They don't have that social conditioning yet that says grown men don't try to sleep out for 300 nights a year. (At least not by choice.) For kids, it's like, Sleep out in the middle of winter under a full moon with coyotes and elk wandering all around? Yes!

And that is what I want, more than anything. Look, I'll admit it: This is a selfish thing. I'm doing this for me. I'm doing this to explore me. And I will also shamelessly admit that this is nothing less than some kind of spiritual quest, some peculiar mid-life rite of passage. I bet if Thoreau or Lao Tsu or Crazy Horse were alive now, they'd be out savoring Ridges Basin in old vans with laptops, too.

But I will just as shamelessly say that this is also my personal peculiar form of parenting. Like any good dad, I want to be a role model. And I like to think that my heading out in a van every night so I can tweak my life a little shows my kids that they, too, can be as different and crazy as they must when they need to no matter what everybody else says, because their dad did it. I figure that the way I'm going, I can raise the bar of what's okay to do high enough so they'll have lots of room to pass under comfortably.

And who knows, maybe with the help of The Project, by their joining me on this zany little venture, they'll figure things out early enough so that they won't have to do crazy things to figure themselves out later. Maybe they'll grow up a good, healthy crazy to begin with.

Silt, sun, and time on the San Juan River

We find our first camp only seven miles or so below the put in, an ominous number as I calculate the long days of floating ahead. This is no matter, though, once the cocktail flag goes up on a blue oar and the cocktail cooler is opened. We'll worry tomorrow, maybe, I think. But I know we really won't worry at all and that I'm just covering my Puritan sense of responsibility if I at least vow to fret.

We mill around the shore of the San Juan River — the "Swan River," the kids call it — under the arms of fat, old, lazy cottonwoods that line the western edge of Comb Ridge, the great slickrock escarpment running from the Abajo Mountains south to Kayenta, Arizona, and made famous as the site of the first attack by the Monkey Wrench Gang in Ed Abbey's novel.

An appropriate location, then. While our expedition's kids stalk lizards, we grownups raise our rum drinks in salute toward the cocktail flag, now a more elaborate red monkey wrench on a black field circled by the statement, "Hayduke Lives." A bit passé of a logo, but not for me. I'm one of those who still finds the Allman Brothers as vital as gasoline for driving, and whose radical roots of river running and suicidal tendency to say what he thinks were birthed in a better, simpler time — the 1980s — when Abbey's monkey wrench was the rallying symbol of wilderness warriors around the West, and we knew who the enemies were: big resource companies and their puppet governors in the BLM, Forest Service, and the National Park Service.

Those were to the good old days. These days, it seems, defenders of wild country have divided into a number of competing marketing niches. Meanwhile, the enemy lies cloaked behind some nebulous dust storm rising from an approaching horizon-to-horizon battle line of pillaging cultural crusaders: an armored division of Realtors in cowboy hats and driving Cadillacs, a battalion of foot soldiers in polo shirts wielding golf clubs, Lycra-clad scouts on mountain bikes, and amphibious teams marching with kayaks over their shoulders and cell phones in their ears. Behind them follow units of support vehicles: road pavers and Starbucks handcarts and Wal-Mart 18-wheelers.

I'd rather battle a land-raping, tree-eating, money-grubbing timber baron any day. But old ways are hard to lose, and so the monkey wrench hangs around as the rallying point of us middle-aged enviromeddlers, as Abbey called us — idealists who trust the compass bearing of our consciences, which were programmed sometime in the mid-to-late Pleistocene, and that tell us that the more our late-20th century culture industrializes, corporatizes, homogenizes, suburbanizes, mechanizes, and generally metastasizes our world, the more freedom we lose. And I mean freedom of choice, but *real* choice: the choice of how to live rather just how to make a living.

Tonight, though, we don't fight; today we enjoy what's here. And so between cocktails, my wife and I take the kids on a scramble up the low ridge behind camp for a look into the long gory gash of Comb Wash. The valley itself is a wide parting of bedrock flesh, exposing a meandering cottonwood-green vein. The east side is Comb Ridge, a ragged and sheer exposure of upended bedrock layers, and the west side is the same rock bent into a steep and water-carved slope called Lime Ridge Anticline.

Sarah and I scale the slickrock up 60 or 70 feet, pushing the kids ahead of us. Just below the top we look up in time to see Webb, arms upraised like a preacher, blurting "It's so *beautiful!*" Sarah shakes her red head, and we laugh as the kids dance away over the knoll like the VonTrapp children. We laugh because this sight is a tad tough to take seriously since that enraptured child is the same little boy who at home refuses to wear anything without either a Colorado Rockies or Batman logo on it. A little silt, sun, and time, though, and he's already another flaming nature boy.

And that is one reason we are on this river trip.

The next morning, we eat, pack, rig, and are off by mid-morning, hoping to put some miles under our tubes. But the river rules, and for the first hour, at least, it dictates that we shall go forth slowly. As the river turns and joins the wide Comb Wash Valley, the stream slows and spreads and braids itself into a maze of islands, sandbars, and channels, forcing us to guess and calculate the deepest routes and to row through its slothful meandering. No problem; we willingly abdicate our fate, and go, as they say, with the flow.

After some while the gentle coast through cottonwood groves and sage flats ends; the river bends west again. We return to canyon country as the river slices a corridor into the sandstone guts of Lime Ridge Anticline. Things change when we slip into the canyon. We enter good ol' redrock country, and the river responds to its new confinement and channeling. Nothing too dramatic or dangerous, but an exhilarating change nonetheless; as the river is funneled between the rock walls it accelerates and trips over itself, stumbling into some low, sloshing waves. The kids hoot and cheer. I pull on the oars, point us into the waves, and our bulky and loaded cataraft rocks and rolls.

Some explanation and scene setting here: A cataraft is a river-version of a sailing catamaran — two 16-foot inflated pontoon tubes connected by frames with no floor, and ours is manufactured right here in the Four Corners area (keep your money at home whenever possible). We also have added our own modification for family travel: an old banquet table is strapped to the front frame, bridging the bows of the two pontoons to create a roomy platform for the kids to sit, read, nap, or, as now, to ride the waves while Sarah holds their lifejackets. At lunch the table whips off and becomes our lunch counter. It's not your catalogue-ordered custom-fit river-gear accessory, but it cost only a six-pack, and I rather like the redneck ambiance it bestows. I think about maybe putting our boat up on blocks in the front yard when we get home.

We plunge on. Around a right-hand bend, into a left turn, and the waves pile higher into curling haystacks that break over bow and onto the table like the tide crashing in. Still no problem; I yank and crank a bit harder on the oars to keep the boat straight and push into each rise to maintain *ooomph* through the growing wave train; the kids still laugh and yelp, and Sarah tightens her grip. But something odd is going on. Saying these waves are growing is more than an expression or even an optical illusion. What on approach are gentle swells or an easy set of rollers definitely rise, then crest, and then surge like watery fists into big back-curling breakers. I find myself straining to bob and weave and keep nosing through them, and still they push our beast of a boat around and stall us on their crests.

No problem, no problem, I say as Sarah looks back a wee bit concerned. I am now thrusting hard on the oars and — wham! — we are kicked sideways as a downstream oar is ripped from my hand and ejected into the current, picking, of course, a speedier route downstream than we are on. I haven't needed a spare oar in ten years, and then on a class IV stretch of water, but I still remember how to whip it out. I free it of its rigging on the side of the tube, and soon we're back in control. Sarah laughs nervously, and the kids just whoop and hoot on, unaware anything significant has happened.

What we're experiencing are the famous (in the circles I hang out in, anyway) San Juan sand waves. A coincidental coordination of streambed slope, sediment texture, and river flow that makes wave forms rise and fall in the river bottom itself. The result on the water's surface is a group of waves thrusting up, growing into big, tight, exaggerated, cresting curlers; after a few minutes of glory, they then recede, shrink, and finally disappear. They can get big, but generally they are more fun than dangerous. Still, they can punch you in the back of your head if you let down your guard.

All things must pass, and so, too, do the sand waves. We soon return to our regularly scheduled program, just floating down yonder banded-rock corridor on the San Juan's liquid conveyor.

Anna looks back at me. "Remember when we were driving in the car, and you said there wouldn't be any big waves on the Swan River?" she asks. She holds me in her sweet-eyes stare, like Cindy-Loo Who smiling up at the Grinch with the Christmas tree over his shoulder.

I remembered. She had asked me last week while we were driving and talking about the upcoming trip.

"No, of course there aren't," I had answered, assuming the posture of the reassuring and confident parent. I smiled at her in the rear-view mirror, nodding wisely.

I must learn to choose my assertions more carefully. Kids, as any parent who has ever made an off-handed promise to one can tell you, are as literal as lawyers, and as uncompromising in their verbal contracts. She says nothing more; point made.

We float on.

Off to the sides of the river, slot canyons cut the tan walls, many of the side-canyons not reaching river level and instead ending ten, twenty, thirty feet overhead in pour offs undercut with alcoves like the indentations of capital domes. It's a green, red, and blue world we're in; even above, cauliflower clouds with bottoms the color of redwood reflect the redrock world below. The kids lie on their bellies on the door-deck watching the water swirl like thin broth. A heron takes off heavily from a boulder in front of us, its spear of a beak the nose cone of a crooked and bend body attached to a monumental wingspan and area. It moves downstream away from us heavily, flopping, flapping, like it's an effort, big *lift ... lift ... lift*s, stick feet trailing awkwardly behind. It looks like another Pleistocene throwback, like it should be jumping off the high rims of glaciers, circling mammoths. Farther downstream, five bighorn sheep graze the boulder fields along shore. Webb sees them first and points them out. We applaud him on his guiding skill, and he glows.

In the afternoon we emerge from this stretch of canyon and into another flatland. As we leave the canyon, its bedrock beds dive (truly a verb in geologic time) back into the earth, giving way to the tablelands that stand in the bowl formed by the Mexican Hat syncline, flat red layers of iron-rich mudstones and sandstones, relatively late layers on the great rock pile that is southeastern Utah. Here in the open we can look across the rusted spires and low walls and see in the far distance the blue-white bands of the great escarpment of Cedar Mesa, 1,500 feet above us and capped with a fuzzy dark piñon-juniper crew-cut top. Closer by the sandstones grow softer and rounded and golden and drape the slopes of nearby hills like fancy gowns. A mining road is etched along the riverside, chocked up with meticulously and laboriously laid stonework; a fool's labor, it seems to me, hand-carting and carving stone and clay to reach a place worthy of gouging a hole in the ground, but still nobler than laboring and building on Wall Street.

But, then again, I am easily amused.

It is the fourth day on the river, and we stop for a walk up an entrenched redrock side canyon sliced into Cedar Mesa. After a while, our party spreads and then dissolves into pairs, and I find myself wading this warm side creek on a slow pace, alone with Anna. Sometimes we hold hands; sometimes she plods ahead to investigate the shallower pools and potholes by herself, curious and only mild cautious about the water's depth, its texture, about whether some unseen creatures lurk under the shimmering surface. We climb the weathered slickrock stair-ways and leave parallel footprints in the sand spread in pockets and mini-ergs by the recent flash floods.

We saunter along at a child's pace, which could be worse. Walking behind a three-foot-tall hiker allows me to absorb myself in the broken country. And to relish the company. We talk little, but we communicate more than we ever have. I hold Anna's little hand between my thumb and forefinger like a precious coin as we stroll together across a ballroom of flat, pock-marked gray sandstone.

This scene isn't composed of much on the surface, just me and my little girl, and the simple fineness of rock and sun, and a silver thread of water. Yet I, here at this moment, am confident and richly content in my gut-solid assertion — not that I am just happy to *be* here (the happiness of the tourist), and not that I am fortunate to *have* this (the arrogance of the environmentalist) — that I *am* this: I am this shattered rock and that sweet wild water and that radiant sun burning through my ratty straw hat, and I am this next little critter who will inherit this big beautiful fatty of a world.

This is my religion: *Nothing is inorganic; everything is animate.*

This is my vision: That we humans, like the earth we are composed of, are just another intriguing and entertaining eddy in the cryptic flow of the elements. And that is enough. That is more than enough mystery and gift to satisfy my senses of meaning and worth.

And this pagan, pantheistic sensibility as old and deep as the human gene pool is what I share with my daughter, maybe not in words (yet), but in our touch, in our walk, and in our venturing here together.

And I realize this is my work: parenting as forging another link in the human chain, and hardening that link with the principles my Pleistocene conscience tells me matter most: appreciating, celebrating, and defending life and land, kin and community, freedom and wildness, self trust and courage and passion — the fuel that for millions of years has burned at the core of the human spirit, and the very things our present culture subverts.

As a parent, I am working to save not just wild nature, but wild human nature. I don't pretend to know where this parenting will lead — parenting is the most uncertain of businesses — and I don't want to tell my kids what to feel. I just want to teach them to trust what *they* feel.

All Sarah and I can really do is escort our kids into the real world — the world that transcends culture — as friends exploring and adventuring together, and encourage them to listen to and act on what their own consciences tell them about that world.

I have, of course, even written this down and tacked it over my desk. On a little piece of paper on which I've scribbled "Ken's Parenting Plan," I've typed it all out. It says:

> *I don't want my kids to fear death;*
> *I definitely don't want them to fear life;*
> *I want them to not fear living,*
> *and to fear not-living.*

It's not always easy — I am drawn to sometimes being too protective, too ready to catch them when they fall, to shield them from the truths of life and living — but I'm trying. Truthfully, parenting is the hardest thing I've ever done. The most demanding, grueling, self-doubting and self-scrutinizing job I've ever taken on. Who am I to teach? To be a role model? To discipline? How do I be policeman and lover all at once, especially knowing that how I walk that balance is shaping forever my relationship to my kids, my kids' relationships to the world, and my kids' relationships to the themselves? How do I let myself still be a real person, to be and become who I am and must be — always best for any true relationship between people, even though it means there will be challenges and conflicts — when it often seems easier to avoid that work by following of some ideal of who I should be? How can I carry that responsibility? How do I do this without losing my mind? Without being drowned by an anchor of self-doubt as I try to swim this turbulent sea of choices and decisions?

To be honest, I still have no answer to those questions. So I do what I do best: act now by gut, then understand later. It's all feel, after all. I did, though, make a vow early on in my parenting career: My goal is not to raise my kids as clones of me — as pagan, or outdoorsy, or environmentalist — but to let them be themselves. I can best do that by being who *I* am, and trust them to understand and follow not what I do, but just the fact I did what is most true to me. And that's why I take them outside, teach them skills; that's why I fight for places to take them outside. My hope — no, my faith — is, maybe if my kids are given choices, they'll make the best ones.

That is the multi-million-year occupation of being a parent. Today, that is monkey-wrenching by parenting.

Anna stands in a shallow pool and steps with that wobbly careful step of a child, experimentally moving out into deeper water, up to her shins, her knees. I squat, ready to spring, but let her go, letting her test and risk ... some. She slips and splashes onto her back, flailing, and I'm on her like a snake strike. She stands with my gentle pull, the back of her short blonde hair dripping, and she scolds me, "I've got it!" I couldn't tell Anna what to do if I wanted to.

I lift her onto my shoulders, her wet legs cooling my chest. We move down canyon toward the rest of our party.

It is our last morning on the river. Under a hot, still sun, the solar stare, we row out onto the river, festive as ever, as charged as ever by that first tug of the current on our tubes. This elation, though, is tempered by the rational knowledge that the retreating beach is our last camp of the trip.

But at least we're still on the river, right?

We pass the first hour or so quietly and diligently at work on our daily river chores — looking around, pointing out curious shapes in the rocks, staring into the river, sniffing the air for scent trails. But our studies soon reveal something different — there are no longer any water sounds. There is current, the channel is still narrow and clearly defined, there are still boulders scattered like shrapnel in the water. But there is no sound — no gurgle, no slosh, no teasing hiss of whitewater approaching around the bend.

Come to think of it, there's no bird song. Just the heavy weight of empty August air. There's still current in the river, yet the changes have begun. The river is slowing, and the channel is starting to spread, the river's edge gnawing away into the shrub-covered shore. The silence, I realize, is just the first sign of fatality, the cessation of breath from a still-warm body. We have reached the upper reaches of Lake Powell, the marketing title for the reservoir flooding Glen Canyon.

Well, we shan't go without a gesture: above our hillbilly boat, the Hayduke Lives flag flutters valiantly in what air movement there is, pressed into service as our Ned Ludd Navy jack. Flying the wrench today is a silly, meaningless, thoroughly ineffectual gesture against something like a 150-mile-long freshwater impoundment, of course, but it's my gesture nonetheless. It's my glare. It's my life in a nutshell.

By mid-afternoon we're definitely on the lake. There is still some lingering current, but it is more of a vague general movement amongst swirls and dead water. The river is stretched flat and thin, running nearly redrock wall to redrock wall — a couple hundred yards across in places. There's no longer any wildlife to see because there's no place to look for it — no riparian habitat, just water and tall rock walls, 400-foot blue-black bathtub sides. So we just stroke on, pulling on the oars as mechanically and thoughtlessly as a politician at a public meeting. Yes, the sights here are still beautiful — it's the same fundamental components of our previous days: rock, water, and sun — but this, nonetheless, is an industrialized landscape. We are outside, but we are not out-of-doors.

Even a kid knows this. Even though we still float through a canyon, Anna turns back to me and asks, "Can we go back to the Swan River sometime?"

I look out over the flat, lake-blue water and taste the bitterness of the dead silence — no canyon wrens, no water sounds, no croaks of herons, not even the hacks of ravens. To my surprise, though, I see one last Pleistocene pagan vision: This is not the silence of death, but the muting of imprisonment. Even though the river is gone for time being, bound and gagged for a while, it's just waiting, on river time.

"You bet we will," I answer Anna.

And when we do, I vow to myself, I'll teach you to see the river under the reservoir, too.